ARGUMENTATION & ADVOCACY

STUDIES IN SPEECH

Consulting Editor | DON GEIGER
University of California, Berkeley

argumentation & advocacy

► RUSSEL R. WINDES
Queens College, The City University of New York

► ARTHUR HASTINGS
Stanford University

RANDOM HOUSE • NEW YORK

Second Printing, May, 1966

© Copyright, 1965, by Random House, Inc.

Library of Congress Catalog Card Number: 65-11867
Manufactured in the United States of America

PREFACE

We believe that argumentation should be taught as a means of discovering and supporting intelligent decisions, both for individuals and for society. A course or book about argumentation should teach the student how to analyze controversies and to formulate propositions which reveal the issues; it should teach the student how to construct arguments from evidence about the controversy; it should instruct him in how to combine and manage arguments to discover answers to the problem which initiated the controversy. As an investigator the student will use these rational processes to discover the best belief to hold or the best action to take on a social issue. But going further, as an advocate he will use these same processes to prove his conclusion to others in his society—however large or small—hoping ultimately to resolve the controversy. This book is an introduction to the principles of argumentation applied to inquiry and advocacy on social issues.

This is not a book on intercollegiate debating. Some books on argumentation are directed principally to the theory and practice of academic debate, where the principles of argumentation are turned to specific applications in tournament debating. Instead we will discuss the role of argumentation in political, economic, cultural, and general social decision-making, where many kinds of conclusions must be drawn and the final decision is made by society itself.

The principles explained in this book will be best learned through practice. So the exercises at the end of each chapter are vital to the usefulness of the ideas. The exercises are planned to force the use of the material in the chapter. As a result they are sometimes difficult to do correctly, because applying the principles of argumentation often requires difficult and complex thinking. This will be discovered by those who for the first time attempt to locate the vital issues of a proposition or accurately state the elements of an argument. But the exercises are exciting as well as instructive, dealing as they do with interesting problems and productive mental processes. There are two general kinds of exercises. One requires the analysis of another person's argument or advocacy, and the other requires creative work on the part of the student. Each serves a different purpose, so both types are important. In addition to these projects, we urge the student to use the principles of argumentation in his own activities—on the job, in groups and organizations, in other classes, and in his advocacy.

In the writing of this book, Mr. Windes had primary responsibility for chapters one through four, and Mr. Hastings for chapters five through seven.

RUSSEL R. WINDES
ARTHUR HASTINGS

CONTENTS

ARGUMENTATION & ADVOCACY

► 1 ◄ THE RATIONAL PROCESSES AND PUBLIC CONTROVERSY IN A FREE SOCIETY

In February of 1945 the Allied governments pledged themselves at Yalta to the use of "democratic means" for the solution of conflicts arising after the close of World War II. The free world did not take long to grasp the fact that the Russian interpretation of "democratic means" was vastly different from the meaning free people attached to the concept. Two years later, February, 1947, United States Secretary of State George Marshall sat through forty-four long sessions at a Big Four foreign ministers conference in Moscow, attempting to work out peace treaties for Germany and Austria through "democratic means." The longer the sessions ground on, and the more impatient Marshall became, the more he sensed the distinction between a free and totalitarian society. Unable to contain his feelings any longer, trying desperately to break through Russian intransigency, Marshall interrupted the forty-fourth session with a lecture to the Russians on the meaning of democracy in a free society. A free society, he insisted, recognizes both the dignity and the sovereignty of the people who compose it. In a democratic society the ultimate power rests with the citizens, who alone can abridge their own rights:

We believe that human beings have certain inalienable rights—that is, rights which may not be given or taken away. They include the right of every individual to develop his mind, and his soul, in the ways of his own choice, free of fear and coercion—provided only that he does not interfere with the rights of others. To us a society is not free if men who respect the rights of their fellow-men are not free to express their own beliefs and convictions without fear that they may be snatched away from their home or family, without fear of being deprived of life, liberty, and the pursuit of happiness. A free society must assure such rights to every individual and effectively prevent any government or group, however powerful or however numerous, from taking such rights away from or imposing any such fears on any individuals, however weak or however few.

After Marshall concluded his remarks, Russian Foreign Minister Molotov commented on the "number of valuable remarks" Marshall had presented and launched a bitter verbal attack on "war-mongering capitalists."

Marshall's eloquent insights harken us back to another day at the close of another bloody battle when Pericles took the occasion of a funeral for those Athenians killed in the Peloponnesian War to give an oration describing the differences between free society in Athens and the totalitarian society of her enemies. Like Marshall, Pericles spoke of the sovereignty of the people. That sovereignty, he maintained, existed only through free knowledge, free expression, and free ballot: "We Athenians are able to judge at all events if we cannot originate, and instead of looking on discussion as a stumbling block in the way of action, we think it an indispensable preliminary to any wise action at all." Athenians, said Pericles, think before they act, and the right to think and to express one's thoughts freely distinguishes the free from the captive society.

THE FREE VERSUS THE
TOTALITARIAN SOCIETY

These reflections serve to introduce the study of advocacy as a rational means through which free society resolves its public controversies and reaches decisions as to matters of public policy. The concepts of free society and free advocacy are both complementary and inseparable. In 1776 Thomas Jefferson expressed his theory of "natural rights" in the Preamble to the Declaration of Independence:

> We hold these Truths to be self-evident, that all Men are created equal, that they are endowed by their Creator with certain unalienable Rights, that among these are Life, Liberty, and the Pursuit of Happiness—That to secure these Rights governments are instituted among Men, deriving their just power from the consent of the governed. . . .

In so writing, Jefferson expressed the foundation for free government: A free government is government by the consent of the governed; the ultimate political power rests in the people who have both the right and the responsibility to direct that government and to change it at any time by peaceful means. The Jeffersonian concept of the "sovereignty of the people" held that power is legitimate only when it is under contract, that is, the people delegate a part of their sovereignty to the government, authority which may be used only so long as the people wish it to be used.

Totalitarian government, on the other hand, is social organization in which the government occupies the totality of the field in every area of the citizen's life. The state is sovereign, not the people, and the people have no *rights*, through peaceful or other means, to direct that government or to change it. One man, or some self-chosen group, holds ultimate sovereignty; there is no contract between him and the people. The relation between leaders and followers is one of force and counter-force, a relation of compulsion on the one hand and submission or resistance on the other. Adolf Hitler described the situation well in *Mein Kampf:* "The State is quite simply the instrument of the nationality, an instrument of power to be used by the governing group."

The difference between free and totalitarian government rests in the principle of the sovereignty of the people. In a free society this principle makes sure that vested interests, power groups, and ruling classes cannot perpetuate themselves in office indefinitely and cannot legislate and enforce their policies interminably. The principle of sovereignty likewise insists that the vested interests, in their attempts to preserve the *status quo,* cannot suppress minority opinion and action through controls over belief and action. If sovereignty rests with all the people, as it does, then it must be held equally by all the people. Accordingly, both majority and minority groups can claim their rightful privileges; neither can be denied individual or collective rights. In totalitarian societies the people have only those privileges which the government from time to time chooses to give.

THE NATURE OF FREE GOVERNMENT

Free people cannot live in anarchy. Government must be formed and laws passed and enforced both in order to protect society from external and internal dangers and in order to promote the general welfare among all people. Therefore, in a free society the people enter a basic compact—they delegate some of their sovereignty to governments (local, state, and national in the case of the United States). At the same time they reserve the right to direct the government in matters of public policy and to change the government if and when it does not respond to their wishes. In short, all matters of public policy shall be decided by corporate action. Policy is enforced by due legal procedure. Those who oppose a policy have the right to work actively for its reversal through peaceful means.

If policy is to reflect the wishes of the people, then free society must provide ways through which the opinions of its citizens, with regard to any issue, can be formulated and communicated to government. Direct democracy is one such means. At the town meeting, for example, all citizens of a community may convene to discuss mutual problems and to advocate solutions to those problems. Conflicts in opinion are resolved through majority vote. Similarly, members of a particular church meet to discuss and advocate various alternatives relating to the hiring of a new minister; the resulting conflict of opinion is resolved through a direct vote of the congregation. Many decisions in a free society are decided through the processes of direct democracy.

But the majority of conflicts which beset mass society cannot be resolved through direct democracy. The citizens of Illinois cannot meet together in Springfield to debate and vote upon a proposed amendment to the state constitution. Consequently, free society has provided itself with a second means of communicating the wishes of its citizens —representative democracy. Representative democracy permits citizens to direct both the broad and the specific policies they wish their government to follow. At regular intervals the people elect public officials who then represent, at various levels of government, the will of those who elect them. Through such elections the people dictate the general direction they wish their government to follow. They vote for representatives who commit themselves, if elected, to a stronger or weaker government, to more or less socialization, to more or less extensive international involvement, to *laissez faire* or planned economy. Between elections, through representative government, citizens make their positions known concerning particular matters of public policy. Through direct communication with their representatives, or through indirect communication, the people continue to specify governmental action on such matters as approving or rejecting a treaty ending atmospheric testing of atomic weapons, lowering taxes or keeping them at the same level, cutting back foreign aid funds or maintaining funds at their present rate, and granting medical care at public expense for those citizens over the age of sixty-five or rejecting such a proposal. Occasionally specific issues become vital campaign issues, as in the case of the monetary issue in 1896 and of the League of Nations in 1920. More often than not, however, this is not the case. What is significant is that in both direct and representative government the sovereign people form their opinions on issues and make their judgments known to a government sensitive to those judgments. Vital to the task of formulating positions on issues as well as the task of making positions known to government is the phenomenon of *public opinion*.

Public opinion is perhaps the most influential force in daily living. It represents the generalized judgment of a considerable number of people on a particular matter of public concern. Every public issue involves conflict, the clashing of different points of view regarding the resolution of the issue. It is the responsibility of government to resolve the conflict in favor of one alternative or another. Through public opinion those who represent the public in government respond both to the seriousness with which citizens regard an issue and to their positions on the various solutions available. Lord Bryce termed public opinion "the great source of power, the master of servants who tremble before it." Government by public opinion exists, Bryce wrote, "where the wishes and views of the people prevail, even before they have been conveyed through the regular law-appointed organs. . . ." Through public opinion the "national will shall be most fully expressed, most quickly known, most unresistingly and cheerfully obeyed."[1]

What is the power that makes public opinion such a potent force? Why do public officials obey the dictates of public opinion so eagerly once they have learned its meaning? Public opinion has influence because it has behind it both the authority of the vote and the so-called voting threat. In expressing their wishes on a public issue, the people in essence tell their representatives: Take the position we want you to take or we will elect somebody else who will. A Congressman who discovers that 86 per cent of his constituents are in favor of low-cost housing will either vote in favor of the low-cost housing bill or make plans for early retirement. A President who discovers the majority of the citizens are against extending diplomatic recognition to Communist China will not undertake to act against the will of the people. The voting threat belongs to the citizen exerting his legal influence on both broad and particular issues of public policy.[2]

The more completely free government prevails in a country, the more the importance of the ability of public opinion to express promptly, fully, and clearly the will of the people on all public issues. Free society has accordingly established criteria for the responsible formulations of public opinion, as well as certain safeguards which prevent governmental interferences that might corrupt the freedom of public opinion. Mr. Justice William O. Douglas addressed himself both to the criteria and the safeguards in a series of lectures delivered at Franklin and Marshall College:

Public opinion—the basis on which our society rests—must be responsible and responsive. To be such it must be disciplined and informed. It cannot be disciplined and informed unless those who shape it have the opportunities for critical inquiry, for the cultivation of open-mindedness, for the search for truth in every recess of the universe. This freedom of inquiry must be allowed to embrace all realms of knowledge—the arts as well as religion and science.[3]

Justice Douglas' "opportunity for critical inquiry" corresponds closely to Thomas Jefferson's concept of the "free marketplace of ideas," a concept which has to be made a reality if public opinion is to fulfill its vital role.

Jefferson's free marketplace assumed that two guarantees were absolutely essential if sovereign people were to direct their government in policy matters: (1) the right of the people to full information on all matters of public policy; (2) the right of freedom to express any opinion on any matter of public concern. The way to prevent illogical and harmful decisions as a result of the pressures of public opinion, wrote Jefferson, was "to give the people full information of their affairs through the channel of the public papers, and to contrive that those papers should penetrate the whole mass of the people." Limiting the freedom of expression, Jefferson also believed, could but have "dangerous results on the sagacity of public opinion." In his First Inaugural he expressed his clear position on free speech: "If there be any among us who wish to dissolve this union, or to change its republican form, let them stand undisturbed, as monuments of the safety with which error of opinion may be tolerated where reason is left free to combat it."

The free marketplace of Jefferson consisted of two processes which were not restricted by governments: the freedom of *inquiry;* the freedom of *advocacy.* Through the processes of inquiry each citizen is guaranteed the right to pursue knowledge on any issue, to investigate any and all sources in order to acquire information, and to discuss that information with others. A government, therefore, cannot restrict the flow of news; it cannot conduct its own actions in secrecy; it cannot censor the nation's press. The citizen has a duty to become knowledgeable on all issues of public policy, a duty both to his government and to his self-interest. But this duty cannot be met unless the citizen possesses the freedom to read wherever his interest and curiosity take him. As Madison wrote, "A people who mean to be their own governors must arm themselves with the power which knowledge gives."

Not only must the citizen have access to information and the freedom to inquire as to its meaning with others, but he must also be guaranteed the right to persuade others to whatever position on any issue he arrives at after due investigation. This is the freedom of advocacy. Public opinion develops as the result of the clash of numerous points of view on any issue. On the issue of stronger v. weaker Federal government, there may be a multitude of diverse opinions. Each citizen, or group of citizens, must test the wisdom of an opinion by advocating that opinion, by putting it up against the opinions of others. Public opinion develops as people attempt to influence the belief of others *through* advocacy and are, in turn, influenced *by* advocacy, by the forceful presentation of the beliefs of other citizens. In such give-and-take, false and dangerous opinions are usually exposed for what they are, although not always. As John Stuart Mill wrote, "The beliefs which we have most warrant for have no safeguard to rest on but a standing invitation to the whole world to prove them unfounded."[4] Eventually the multitude of diverse opinions are reduced to only a few alternatives, often only two. Through advocacy the remaining alternatives are debated freely until public opinion dictates a final choice.

To secure this free marketplace of inquiry and advocacy, the citizen must rely on the guarantees of the First Amendment to the Constitution.

THE FREEDOM OF EXPRESSION

> This is true liberty, when free-born men,
> Having to advise the public, may speak free,
> Which he who can, and will, deserves high praise;
> Who neither can nor will, may hold his peace;
> What can be juster in a State than this?
> (EURIPIDES, *The Suppliants*)

The First Amendment to the Constitution of the United States protects without qualification the free marketplace. It states without ambiguity: "Congress shall make no law respecting an establishment of religion, or prohibiting the free exercise thereof; or abridging the freedom of speech, or of the press; or the right of the people peaceably to assemble, and to petition the Government for a redress of grievances."

Once free people have the right and responsibility to direct their government through the ballot and public opinion, the freedom of expression becomes *sine qua non,* for such freedom protects both their access to knowledge and their right to express that knowledge and opinions growing from it. Freedom of expression is the only guarantee that the people will be kept adequately informed, that they will be allowed to confront all opinion in the attempt to discern truth, and that they may engage themselves freely in the attempt to influence others.

The First Amendment provides that all citizens should have freedom to search for the answers to the problems of social life and to form individual and collective opinions about them. The First Amendment promises that once positions on problems have been formulated, all citizens should have the freedom to express those opinions in any form they wish—through writing, through speaking, through music, drama, and art. Mr. Justice Douglas spoke lucidly of the implications:

. . . there is no free speech in the full meaning of the term unless there is freedom to challenge the very postulates on which the existing regime rests. It is my belief that our First Amendment must be placed in that broad frame of reference and construed to permit even discourse or advocacy that strikes at the very foundation of our institutions. The First Amendment was a new and bold experiment. It staked everything on unlimited public discussion. It chose among conflicting values, selecting the freedom to talk, to argue, and to advocate as a preferred right. It placed us on the side of free discussion and advocacy, come what may.[5]

Every advocate has the responsibility of knowing for himself the allowances and the limitations of the First Amendment. The scope of that amendment has evolved through court decisions rendered mainly during the past fifty years. Until World War I, with the exception of the period of the Alien and Sedition Acts, there was no great public concern over the interpretation of the First Amendment. But the hysteria associated with war led to attempts on the part of both federal and state governments to suppress the freedom of expression. The courts had generally assumed three limitations on the freedom of expression: (1) Expression could be limited when it inflicted injury on another person (libel, defamation); (2) expression could be limited when it endangered law and order and the security of the government; (3) expression could be limited when it undermined social morality. But specific applications had not been spelled out clearly before 1917, particularly in terms of limitations imposed by the latter two criteria. Several thousand prosecutions and judicial proceedings involving freedom of expression emerged from the World War I period and the early 1920's. During this time many states passed laws which sought the punishment of those advocating extreme radicalism. Several constitutional questions presented themselves in these cases: (1) What kinds of free expression constitute a threat to the "security" of the United States? (2) Since the First Amendment prohibits Congress from abridging free expression, does the same restriction apply to the various states? (3) Does freedom of speech also include the freedom of the press? (4) Does freedom of speech also include freedom to peacefully assemble and petition the government for redress of grievances?

In a series of decisions beginning in 1919, the Supreme Court established a more firm legal basis for the First Amendment.[6]

In the *Schenck* decision (249 US 47) Mr. Justice Holmes defined the limits of freedom of expression:

The most stringent protection of speech would not protect a man in falsely shouting fire in a theatre and causing panic. It does not even protect a man from an injunction against uttering words that may have all the effect of force. . . . The question in every case is whether the words used are used in such circumstances and are of such a nature as to create a clear and present danger that will bring about the substantive evils that Congress has a right to prevent.

In 1925 in *Gitlow v. New York* (286 US 652) the Court ruled that the First Amendment was applicable equally to state governments and Federal government. In this decision the Court expanded the term "liberty" in the Fourteenth Amendment ("Nor shall any state deprive any person of . . . liberty . . . without due process of law.") to include "freedom of speech." The Court declared, "We may and do assume that freedom of speech and of the press . . . are among the fundamental personal rights and liberties protected . . . from impairment by the states."

Freedom of speech was clearly broadened to include the freedom of the press, and the freedom of the press was made directly applicable to the states through the Fourteenth Amendment in the *Near v. Minnesota* decision in 1931 (238 US 697). Mr. Justice Hughes wrote the majority opinion: "The fact that the liberty of the press may be abused by miscreant purveyors of scandal does not make any the less necessary the immunity of the press from previous restraint. . . ." And in *DeJonge v. Oregon* (299 US 353), the rights of peaceful assembly and petition were added to those liberties which the state cannot take away. Again Mr. Justice Hughes wrote the majority opinion:

The greater the importance of safeguarding the community from incitements to the overthrow of our institutions by force and violence, the more imperative is the need to preserve inviolate the constitutional rights of free speech, free press, and free assembly in order to maintain the opportunity for free political discussion, to the end that government may be responsive to the will of the people and that changes, if desired, may be obtained by peaceful means.

From these legal bases for the First Amendment, the advocate in American society derives necessary benefits. Through denotations of the meaning of free expression, the public is assured of access to the information that may be needed to form opinions on public issues; at the same time the public is guaranteed the right to engage in free and almost unrestricted inquiry and advocacy relating to those issues. Thus a situation exists in which public opinion *can* responsibly form and clearly make its wishes known.

Freedom of expression, moreover, serves to elicit and encourage all ideas and opinions, no matter how radical or unjust and unsound they may seem at the time. Yesterday's radical idea more than occasionally proves to be today's answer to a probing problem. The platform of Norman Thomas, radical in the 1920's, became a part of the New Deal in the crisis of the 1930's. Clarence Darrow emphasized this benefit in his final plea in defense of twenty Communists charged with advocating the overthrow of the government by force in 1920:

. . . above everything else on earth men should cling fast to their right to examine every question, to listen to everyone . . . to hear the spoken words and read the written words; because if you shut men's mouths and paralyze their minds, then the greatest truth that is necessary for the welfare of the human race may die.

Freedom of expression is finally the minority advocate's great weapon to wage reform, to limit the policies of the majority, and to become eventually himself a part of the majority. With free expression, minorities can and do wage campaigns to educate the public to their beliefs and to persuade the public to accept their positions. Such campaigns temper the policies of the majority, and, on occasion, may result in replacing the majority. The Court suggested this fact in the decision in the *Terminiello* case (337 US 1):

A function of free speech . . . is to invite dispute. It may indeed best serve its high purpose when it induces a condition of unrest, creates dissatisfaction with conditions as they are, or even stirs people to anger. Speech is often provocative and challenging. It may strike at prejudice and preconceptions and have profound unsettling effects as it presses for acceptance of an idea.

WEAKNESSES OF DEMOCRATIC CONFLICT RESOLUTION

In a very real sense the previous discussion on the ways a free society resolves its conflicts and reaches decisions on matters of public policy represents the idealization of the concepts of Jefferson. No one must assume that such concepts are always operative or that they eternally function as they were intended to function, for the betterment of society. Among others, Walter Lippmann has pointed to the "plight of the modern democracies," analyzing that plight as a serious one due primarily to the "practical failures" of the system as opposed to its theoretical constructs. These failures should give cause for concern to all citizens, particularly those who have committed themselves to a study of argumentation and advocacy. Lippmann has suggested an unfortunate tendency to regard free government as inordinately strong, able to withstand assaults from without as well as within. The tendency is unfortunate in that the ideals which form the foundation for free government are no stronger than the will of a people to implement them through dedication and action. The American people are not always willing to do just that.[7]

There are at least four serious insecurities associated with democracy's decision-making: apathy, ignorance, intolerance, and the threat of laws and actions which strike at the heart of free expression.

Of these four insecurities apathy is perhaps the most insidious, an apathy which allows citizens to presume security, an apathy which continuously suggests that *others* should concern themselves with public issues. As a result, too many citizens refuse to concern themselves with a public controversy until it is too late for their opinion to make any difference in its resolution. It is all too easy not to take the trouble to inform oneself about a public problem, and advocating a position on the problem takes a great deal of time. Apathy sees to it that more than half the eligible voters stay away from the polls at many elections. Apathy makes sure that either public opinion does not form on any problem or that the public opinion that forms has little force behind it. Pericles was likewise concerned with public apathy; he declared the man who takes no interest in the affairs of society to be not merely useless, but worse yet, dangerous.

Even if people should concern themselves over a public controversy, that concern alone is not sufficient. Along with concern goes the responsibility of making oneself knowledgeable, of making oneself qualified to examine various alternatives to the solution of a problem in order to arrive at positions on those alternatives. If public opinion is not based on thorough analysis of an issue and the support of a resulting position through evidence and reasoning, then that opinion may be not only worthless but pernicious. Witch-hunting in the seventeenth century represented a certain public opinion, opinion based on false information and indefensible analysis. Witch-hunting still exists.

Intolerance and self-righteousness go hand in hand to weaken the effectiveness of inquiry and advocacy. Bigotry, an unwillingness to accept or even listen to a different point of view, slowly but surely closes the mind to both reason and change. Intolerance abhors change, despises new ideas, hates that which smacks of non-conformity. The political bigot, the religious bigot, and the social bigot, like the totalitarian ruler, would preclude if they could all expression which would threaten the security of their own points of view. They assume themselves to be the only judges of certainty, and they seek to impose their standards on society. They become, in the words of Eric Hoffer, the "true believers." Justice Learned Hand forcefully attacked such intolerance and bigotry in his famous speech in front of the New York Board of Regents, October 24, 1952:

I believe that that community is already in process of dissolution where each man begins to eye his neighbor as a possible enemy, where non-conformity with the accepted creed, political as well as religious, is a mark of disaffection; where denunciation, without specification or backing, takes the place of evidence; where orthodoxy chokes freedom of dissent; where faith in the eventual supremacy of reason has become so timid that we dare not enter our convictions in the open lists, to win or lose. Such fears as these are a solvent which can eat out the cement that binds the stones together; they may in the end subject us to a despotism as evil as any that we dread. . . . The mutual confidence on which all else depends can be maintained only by an open mind and a brave reliance upon free discussion. I do not say that these will suffice; who knows but we may be on a slope which leads down to aboriginal savagery. But of this I am sure: if we are to escape, we must not yield a foot upon demanding a fair field and an honest race to all ideas. Blame not before thou has examined; understand first and then rebuke. Answer not before thou has heard. . . .[8]

Equally the enemy of democratic decision-making, and often originating from apathy, ignorance, and intolerance, are attempts to curb free expression and inquiry through laws and concerted parochial public opinion. As noted both in the *DeJonge* and *Near v. Minnesota* cases, legislatures, in their fear of the power of certain ideas, will not only attempt to curb overt action stemming from the expression of those ideas, but will attempt to curb the right to express those ideas. The state of Oregon attempted to remove DeJonge's right of free speech because he wished to advocate a political philosophy not in keeping with what it held to be "right." In the *Near* case, the state of Minnesota attempted to forbid the publication of future issues of a newspaper because it held the paper to be "malicious, scandalous, and defamatory." To be sure, these cases were some years ago, but the dangers represented still persist, as evidenced by *Dennis v. United States* (341 US 494); *Feiner v. New York* (340 US 315); *Watkins v. United States* (354 US 178); and *Barenblatt v. United States* (360 US 109).

Dangers coming from the tyranny of a majority seeking to impose its views on the minority are likewise disturbing. A majority must respect minority groups, and most often in a free society this is the case. But there are times when the majority not only opposes the minority viewpoint, but seeks to suppress or even exterminate it altogether. Hence, a Clarence Darrow could vividly recall the persecutions he underwent as an agnostic child in a theistic community, or the plight of minority union members in an anti-labor society at the turn of the century. Racial, religious, moral, economic, and political persecutions throughout history have aimed at the destruction of the rights of those who dissent, and the chief among these rights has always been free expression. Such persecutions, not always sanctioned by law, have the same force of law.

As previously noted, there are generally recognized at least three areas in which some control over free expression can be exercised by society: when expression inflicts injury on another individual; when expression threatens the security of government; when expression is thought to undermine social morality. Laws of libel are rarely repressive in terms of the function of the free marketplace. Laws relating to censorship of literature and motion pictures may be odious to liberals by their very nature, but there is doubt that they seriously restrict the citizen's right to know. The most serious threats to the free marketplace, and hence democratic decision-making, appears to be presented by interpretations given to the "clear and present danger" concept of Mr. Justice Holmes.

The rule of thumb established in the *Schenck* case has been that the government is justified in curbing freedom of expression only when it can be proven that the expression constitutes a "clear and present danger" to law and order, i.e., the security of the government. Some would argue that anyone who advocates publicly any anti-constitutional doctrine is thereby creating a "clear and present danger." Mr. Justice Douglas has stated the opposite point of view:

From *Schenck to Dennis,* I know of no abridgement of freedom of expression which was properly sustained under the "clear and present danger" test. Being of the generation of young men called to the service in World War I, I cannot conceive that the pamphlets which Schenck distributed had any measurable effect on the conduct of the war effort. Being close to American affairs in the 1950's, I cannot conceive that the communist's advocacy of the violent overthrow of government has convinced more than a handful of the American public. "Clear and present danger" has become merely a convenient excuse for suppression. Yet in my view the only time suppression is constitutionally justified is where speech is so closely brigaded with action that it is in essence a part of an overt act.[9]

Mr. Justice Douglas echoed the words of Mr. Justice Brandeis in his majority opinion in the case of *Whitney v. California* (285 US 514): ". . . no danger flowing from speech can be deemed clear and present, unless the incidents of the evil apprehended are so imminent that they may befall before there is opportunity for free discussion. If there then be the opportunity to expose . . . the falsehood and fallacies . . . the remedy to be applied is more speech, not enforced silence."

What is vital to the advocate, perhaps, is not that everyone shall speak at any time he pleases, saying anything he pleases, but that everything worth saying shall be said. Although citizens may be on many other grounds prevented from speaking, they should never be prevented because their views are considered to be false or dangerous. No idea should be outlawed because someone in command thinks it unwise, unfair, or even un-American. No advocate should be declared out of order because the majority disagrees with what he intends to say. All ideas must have a hearing—the wise and the unwise, the dangerous and the safe, the American and the un-American. It is the destruction of the thinking process of society against which the First Amendment is directed. The First Amendment rests on the assumptions that people are capable of governing themselves, that people are concerned about their society sufficiently to make themselves knowledgeable on the public questions. It rests on the assumption that the widest possible dissemination of information from diverse and antagonistic sources is essential to the welfare of successful conflict resolution.

THE RATIONAL PROCESSES
AND PUBLIC CONTROVERSY

The focus of this book is on the rational processes of advocacy and how those processes function in a free society to resolve the infinite number of controversies which arise over matters of public policy. We have already seen that the survival of free institutions depends on the opportunity and the ability of sovereign people to make responsible decisions in social matters. We have observed that opportunity and ability depend on the constitutional guarantees of a free marketplace, as well as the concern free people demonstrate in public affairs and their willingness to knowledgeably participate in the decision-making process. Assuming that freedom of the marketplace *is* assured and that people *do* interest themselves sufficiently on public problems to possess knowledgeable opinions, through what means, then, must they go about resolving public problems?

There are basically two approaches to the resolution of conflict, the *irrational* and the *rational* approaches. People often reach decisions irrationally. Matters of personal concern may be privately resolved through the uncontrolled influence of emotion, the influence of an authority, the influence of group pressures, and so forth. Matters of public concern are too frequently resolved in similar ways. A mob may irrationally reach a decision which results in lawless violence; a frightened public may react to a problem in such an emotional manner that a hurried decision may strike at the roots of free government; social pressures of conformity may force the acceptance of an alternative to a problem by people who have reason to doubt the wisdom of the alternative. Social groups may attempt to solve a problem by avoiding the problem altogether, rationalizing various reasons for such an avoidance. These irrational approaches to conflict resolution often lead to errors, mistakes, even blunders and tragedies. History abounds with decisions made irrationally: the war with Mexico, 1848; the Spanish-American War, 1898; the rejection of the League of Nations, 1919-1920; the failure to react to the menace of the dictators, 1935-1938; general disarmament following World War II; the suppression of minority thought during the McCarthy era, 1950-1954. In these cases, and in thousands of others, decisions were made irrationally, through reliance on fear, desire, pride, influence of authority, intuition, ignorance, prejudices, rationalizations, and so forth.

The concept of free government provides a far better means of reaching public decisions, the *rational* approach. *Rational processes* incorporate many of the concepts we have already discussed in this chapter—access to information, freedom of expression, concern over public policy as seen in participation in inquiry and advocacy, and the avoidance of intolerance, self-righteousness, and bigotry.

Why does the use of rational processes guarantee better decision-making? Precisely for the many reasons we have already examined in this chapter, and because through the use of rational means the possible use of irrational approaches is excluded. Rational decision-making emphasizes the fact that wise decisions ordinarily require time and patience, time to investigate problems thoroughly, the time to analyze alternatives carefully, and the time to prepare cogent arguments for and against each alternative; the patience to listen to opposing points of view, the patience to suspend judgment until all pertinent arguments have been heard, and the patience to let public opinion gradually inform itself and make itself known to representatives. Rational decision-making respects the rights and dignity of all citizens, the minority no less than the majority; it insists that no problem of public policy should be resolved until all that should be heard about it has been heard and weighed carefully. Such processes may be painfully slow, but that very slowness insures against injurious and dangerous alternatives.

Inquiry and *advocacy* are the essential tools of rational deliberation. Inquiry is substantially a means of the investigation of a problem. Through inquiry the citizen formulates the meaning and significance of a public problem. This is to say, as we shall see in the following chapter, the citizen becomes aware of the existence of a problem in society, which problem he feels to be significant enough to warrant public concern. The problem may concern whether or not his country is sufficiently defended, whether or not his child is sufficiently educated, whether or not his family and friends have medical care, whether or not his community has proper police protection. This awareness is followed by an investigation of the problem itself to discover its seriousness and its consequences; the citizen reads all he can about the problem; he discusses it with friends; he formulates some tentative answers or solutions to the problem which are also topics for discussion with friends and associates. He tries to find others who share his concern over the problem, and in the process of doing so begins to create and develop public opinion about the problem.

Once public opinion has been formed to some degree, once people begin to arrive at positions concerning how the problem is to be solved, *advocacy* becomes a significant part of the rational process and the citizen becomes not so much an *inquirer* as he is an *advocate*. Advocacy has as its primary task the influencing of the belief and behavior of other people. It is the advocate's job to persuade others as to the seriousness of a problem, i.e., to get others to recognize the existence of a problem, as well as to persuade others that the advocate's solution to the problem is a wise and workable one which should be adopted. The advocate, accordingly, is concerned with influence and power; he wants to be effective, to be able to influence person A to accept solution X when otherwise A might accept solution Y or no solution at all.

In the task of influencing others, the advocate may employ a variety of approaches, but essentially he has access to two broad types: the *logical,* or *rational,* and the *psychological.* He may use each approach separately or use them both together. Both, if legitimately and ethically used, constitute the *rational processes of decision-making,* as opposed to the irrational.

The logical approach to advocacy includes the discipline of *argumentation* and argumentative analysis. Classically, argumentation has been listed as one of the four types of discourse: narration, description, explanation, and argumentation. Most popular definitions of argumentation make it a part of the area of persuasion, with its function that of influencing belief and action. While it is true that the eventual findings of argumentative analysis will be used to influence others, it is not true that this is the purpose of argumentation. Argumentation itself does not seek to persuade anybody of anything. *Argumentation functions to discover and formulate the requirements of proof for a proposition or a conclusion.* Through argumentative analysis the advocate discovers what is *logically necessary* to prove whatever proposal or conclusion he believes. He must then employ these findings from argumentation, along with other primarily psychological forms of proof, in an attempt to persuade an audience that his conclusion or proposal should be accepted. Argumentative analysis is thus independent of both audience and advocate; it focuses on a proposition or conclusion strictly in terms of finding out what is logically or sensibly necessary to verify the accuracy and wisdom of the conclusion. What the advocate discovers may influence an audience sufficiently so that the audience will accept the conclusion; logically argumentative analysis should be the sole criterion on which the audience will base its decision. But audiences do not always react in a purely logical manner. Every audience has its own needs, emotions, and values, and these psychological factors impinge severely at times on whether or not that audience will agree to a conclusion solely because it has been logically arrived at and logically presented. Consequently, the advocate incorporates the results of his argumentative analysis into the persuasive advocacy which he presents to his audience. In other words, advocacy consists both of the results of logical or argumentative analysis of a proposal or conclusion as well as the psychological analysis of the conclusion or proposal as it relates to the needs, emotions, and values of his audience. His emphasis will properly be, of course, on the results of his argumentative analysis, for this is what "makes sense" to him and what should be therefore most influential in dealing with an audience. But he will not neglect whatever analysis is necessary to make his arguments *persuasive,* that is, believable.

The psychological approach to advocacy asks the question: How does the advocate persuade a given audience at a given time as to the validity of a conclusion arrived at through argumentative or logical analysis? The advocate's job is to make his arguments acceptable to those who are asked to pass judgment on them. To do this the advocate must be a student of human behavior; he must be aware of the impact of emotions and desires and values on both individuals and groups. He must realize that often psychological factors prevent an individual or groups of individuals from agreeing to a proposal that seems logically sound to the advocate. Attempting to convince certain groups of people that the desegregation of public institutions and facilities in the United States should proceed at all due speed, the advocate would be severely handicapped, no matter how rational the arguments in favor of the proposal might be, by the psychological blocks in the form of fears, anxieties, and accepted values placed in the way of influence by those groups of people. As a result, the advocate, although not abandoning his logical analysis at all, would attempt to adapt that analysis to the emotional involvement of his given audience. In doing so, he would not forsake his own values, but rather, by making his arguments psychologically persuasive, he would assure himself of at least a fair hearing.

Advocacy occurs in many forms, both formal and informal. Informally one advocates his conclusions to his friends, family, and associates as he communicates with them. Students meet over coffee after class to "argue" about a lecture they just heard; two office workers discuss various public issues while driving home from work; construction workers advocate their conclusions about a forthcoming political election during lunch hour; two professors engage in heated controversy over their philosophy of teaching.

Formally, on broader matters of public policy, advocacy takes place when a civic club attempts to decide whether or not to endorse a candidate for mayor and various members make their conclusions known. A church may disagree over the site of a new building and members of the congregation will express their proposals. A faculty senate may consider the matter of a new humanities curriculum and listen patiently while senators express and defend their conclusions. A city council may differ among its members concerning the advisability of changing zoning ordinances, and council members will advocate their opinions. The hypothesis behind all advocacy is that prudent resolution of all public controversy is best arrived at in a situation where opposing parties are given opportunity forcefully to present their alternatives and to defend those alternatives when they are attacked by others. Basic to this point of view is the premise that rational decisions are best and that advocacy tests the rationality of all decisions.

One formal form of advocacy is *public debate*. Debate is advocacy in which opposing or alternate positions are presented to an audience under formalized rules. Debate consists of opposing arguments on a particular proposition or conclusion between a supporting affirmative and an opposing negative. This debate is held according to certain rules of procedure and codes of fair dealing and fair comment to which both parties agree prior to the debate. An affirmative proposes a change in belief and/or action, and a negative both defends existing belief and/or action, and, at the same time, rejects the wisdom behind the affirmative proposal. There are many forms of public debate. Through legislative debate, Congress and the state legislature determine whether or not a proposed bill shall become a law, thus resolving the conflict of a matter of public controversy. Through judicial debate—the presentation of an indictment by the prosecution and the answering of the indictment by the defense—courts of law decide on the innocence or guilt of the accused. Through academic, or educational, debate students are taught both the logical and the psychological processes and their use through advocacy. Debate, then, is a form of advocacy, dealing essentially with the more serious and widespread conflicts over public policy. Debate insures the presentation of at least two alternatives to a controversy, as each advocate presents the strongest possible case for or against a proposal or a conclusion. A voting body then renders a decision, resolving the conflict in favor of one alternative or another.

All advocacy, of course, is not orally presented, although it is often regarded as such. Written advocacy is not only carried on extensively in free society, it is an intrinsic part of society's decision-making. As a matter of fact, much oral advocacy stems from written advocacy. Who can effectively assess the impact of the written advocacy of Thomas Paine or John Dickinson on the events culminating in American independence? Who can properly estimate the influence of the writings of Lovejoy, Garrison, and Stowe on the eventual abolition of slavery? Who could deny the significance of the advocacy of Mary Baker Eddy or of the muckraking of Lincoln Steffens, Ida Tarbell, or Ray Stannard Baker? There is no doubt concerning the persuasiveness of the written word. The discussions of this book are in many ways applicable to both spoken and written advocacy.

Free government cannot function without free inquiry and free advocacy; at the same time, without the backing of free government, inquiry and advocacy are digital exercises at best. Advocacy must have substance and the right to search for truth.

To perceive more acutely these links one need only imagine society without freedom of inquiry and advocacy. As a matter of fact, one need not imagine. In every community there are unmistakable examples of the authoritarian settlement of controversies through either no advocacy at all or through limited and superficial confrontation. Public opinion in such cases is meaningless. It is not at all unusual for a community to discover new policies and laws instituted by its government without benefit of public debate on the appropriateness of those laws. A censorship board may begin censoring community movies and books; a public school may adopt an eleven-month term; a new freeway may consume blocks of residential housing; public utility rates may increase; gasoline taxes may go up. The fault may well lie with an apathetic public, or it may rest with a government that either fears public debate or does not respect the people enough to allow debate.

Nor is the situation confined to local communities. The Eighteenth Amendment to the Constitution, prohibiting the manufacture and sale of intoxicating beverages, was enacted during wartime emotionalism after only perfunctory and brief debate in both Congress and the state legislatures. Most people today recognize the futility of this attempt to legislate morality. Much of the early New Deal legislation was enacted during the famous "100 Days" in 1933 in an atmosphere of rush and frenzy which precluded any real debate. Congress passed bill after bill solely on the recommendation of the President, often with no opportunity at all even to read a bill, much less comprehend its full significance. Small wonder many measures later had to be rewritten because they were discovered to be unworkable, ineffective, or plainly unconstitutional.

Perhaps the events of 1933 are understandable in terms of the grave emergencies of that year. But events of 1963, representing similar suspension of free advocacy, suggest strongly that 1933 was not so exceptional after all. In the winter and spring of 1963, certain groups in the United States attempted to secure the passage of proposed amendments to the Constitution, which would have, if ratified, radically changed constitutional government in the United States. One of the amendments would have created a Court of the Union consisting of the chief justices of the fifty states, with authority to review Supreme Court decisions relating to rights reserved to the states under the Constitution. A second amendment would have removed from the jurisdiction of the Supreme Court matters pertaining to apportionment of state legislatures. A third, the most important, would have amended the amending clause of the Constitution to deprive Congress of any significant role in the amending process, including the capacity to bring about a national debate on any proposed amendment, giving all power to state legislatures to propose as well as to ratify amendments.

Whether by design or by accident, these amendments were introduced in state legislatures with practically no publicity. In many instances, they were voted on by legislators after virtually no debate. As a result, the public had little opportunity to make itself knowledgeable on the amendments, much less to form opinions and make those opinions known to their representatives. Within five months of their introduction, the first amendment had been adopted by four states, the second by thirteen states, the third by eleven. The nature of the amendments prompted Professor Charles L. Black of the Yale Law School to declare that they threatened the "subversion of that balance in Federal-State relations which has . . . enabled us to escape the evils of despotism and totalitarianism. . . ."[10] Under the third proposed amendment, Black observed, a minority of the people could impose any constitutional amendment on the majority.

While no one would deny the right of any group to propose any amendment to the Constitution, every citizen should object to the lack of opportunity to mobilize public opinion on the three proposed amendments through inquiry and advocacy. The example is a striking illustration of what can happen when the marketplace is closed.

This book is concerned with the rational processes as applied to the resolution of public controversies. Such rational processes include the meaning and function of public propositions, the analysis of those propositions to determine their requirements for proof, and the support of conclusions drawn from analysis through evidence and reasoning. Such rational processes also include adapting the results of argumentative analysis to the requirements involved in influencing a given audience, i.e., a persuasive analysis and proof and the ability to attack and defend arguments.

Walter Lippmann has perhaps best summarized the mood of this introductory chapter:

Yet when genuine debate is lacking, freedom of speech does not work as it is meant to work. It has lost the principle which regulates it and justifies it—that is to say, dialectic conducted according to the rules of evidence and logic. If there is no effective debate, the unrestricted right to speak will unloose so many propagandists, procurers, and panderers upon the public that sooner or later in self-defense the people will turn to the censors to protect them. An unrestricted and unregulated right to speak cannot be maintained. It will be curtailed for all manner of reasons and pretexts, and to serve all kinds of good, foolish, or sinister ends.

For in the absence of debate unrestricted utterance leads to the degradation of opinion. By a kind of Gresham's law the more rational is overcome by the less rational, and the opinions that will prevail will be those which are held most ardently by those with the most passionate will. For that reason the freedom to speak can never be maintained merely by objecting to interference with the liberty of the press, of printing, of broadcasting, of the screen. It can be maintained only by promoting debate.

In the end what men will most ardently desire is to suppress those who disagree with them, and, therefore, stand in the way of the realization of their desires. Thus, once confrontation in debate is no longer necessary, the toleration of all opinions leads to intolerance. Freedom of speech, separated from its essential principle, leads through a short transitional chaos to the destruction of freedom of speech.[11]

►NOTES◄

1. James Bryce, *The American Commonwealth* (New York: The Macmillan Company, 1897), pp. 263-265.
2. For additional information on the role of public opinion see: Emory S. Bogardus, *The Making of Public Opinion* (New York: Association Press, 1951); R. M. Maciver, *The Web of Government* (New York: The Macmillan Company, 1947); Bernard Berelson, Paul Lazarsfeld, William McPhee, *Voting: A Study of Opinion Formation* (Chicago: The University of Chicago Press, 1954); William Albright, "Two Decades of Opinion Study," *Public Opinion Quarterly* (Spring, 1957), pp. 14-23.

3. William O. Douglas, *The Right of the People* (Garden City, N. Y.: Doubleday & Company, Inc., 1958), p. 27.

4. John Stuart Mill, "Of the Liberty of Thought and Discussion," in *Utilitarianism, Liberty, and Representative Government* (London: J. M. Dent & Sons, Ltd., 1910), pp. 78-114.

5. Douglas, *op. cit.*, p. 18.

6. For additional study of the evolution of the legal bases for freedom of speech see: Zechariah Chafee, Jr., *Free Speech in the United States* (Cambridge, Mass.: Harvard University Press, 1954).

7. Walter Lippmann, *The Public Philosophy* (Boston: Little, Brown and Company, 1955), Chapters 1 and 2.

8. Learned Hand, *The Spirit of Liberty* (New York: Vintage Books, 1959), p. 216.

9. Douglas, *op. cit.*, pp. 53-54.

10. Walter Lippmann, "The Assault on the Union," *Newsweek* (June 10, 1963), p. 25.

11. Lippmann, *The Public Philosophy*, pp. 129-130.

► E X E R C I S E S ◄

1. Walter Lippmann has written, "The notion that public opinion can and will decide all issues is in appearance very democratic. In practice it undermines and destroys democratic government. For when everyone is supposed to have a judgment about everything, nobody in fact is going to know much about anything. . . . The only effect of inviting everybody to judge every public question is to confuse everybody about everything." (*The Essential Lippmann,* New York: Random House, Inc., 1963, p. 98). Compare this Lippmann conclusion with the conclusions we reach on the role of public opinion in Chapter One. Prepare and present a speech defending or attacking Mr. Lippmann's position.

2. This chapter has mentioned instances in history of great decisions being made without benefit of thoughtful public debate. Find additional historical decisions in which debate was either truncated or suspended. Was each decision less wise in the long run because of the absence of advocacy? Prepare an oral report on one such decision, analyzing the process by which the decision was made and its consequences.

3. The following speeches and essays comment upon the relationship between free government, public opinion, and advocacy:

   a. Thomas Erskine, "Speech for the Defendant in the Trial of Thomas Paine for a Libel, in Publishing *The Rights of Man*," in Chauncey A. Goodrich (ed.), *Select British Eloquence* (Indianapolis: The Bobbs-Merrill Company, 1963), pp. 761-766.

   b. John Stuart Mill, "Of the Liberty of Thought and Discussion," in *Utilitarianism, Liberty, and Representative Government* (London: J. M. Dent & Sons, Ltd., 1910), pp. 78-114.

   c. Alexander Meiklejohn, "The Rulers and the Ruled," in *Political Freedom* (New York: Harper & Row, Publishers, 1960), pp. 8-29.

   d. John Milton, *Areopagitica* (1644).

   e. Theodore Dwight Weld, "A Statement on Lane Seminary," in *The Emancipator* (January 6, 1835), Vol. III, No. 1, p. 1.

   f. Jacques Maritain, "The Rights of the Human and Civic Person," in *The Rights of Man and Natural Law* (New York: Charles Scribner's Sons, 1943), Chapter 1.

   Prepare a short talk critically appraising the relationships established by one or more of the above spokesmen.

4. *Constitutional Law: Cases and Other Problems* (Boston: Little, Brown and Company, 2nd ed., 1961, Vol. II) by Freund, Sutherland, Howe, and Brown presents a number of legal cases in the area of free speech.

Choose one case from among the following and study it thoroughly:

a. *Schenck v. United States,* 1378 ff.
b. *Abrams v. United States,* 1380 ff.
c. *Gitlow v. New York,* 1384 ff.
d. *Whitney v. California,* 1390 ff.
e. *Near v. Minnesota,* 1398 ff.
f. *Bryant v. Zimmerman,* 1430 ff.
g. *Dennis v. United States,* 1523 ff.
h. *DeJonge v. Oregon,* 1433 ff.
i. *Terminiello v. City of Chicago,* 1501 ff.
j. *Feiner v. New York,* 1509 ff.
k. *Thomas v. Collins,* 1439 ff.
l. *Public Utilities Co. v. Pollack,* 1500 ff.
m. *Yates v. United States,* 1540 ff.

Then (1) present, in the form of a brief, the most effective arguments you can for a reconsideration of the case; (2) present an alternative opinion (either a concurring or dissenting opinion) on the case. The presentations should be confined by the facts, in so far as they are revealed in the existing opinions, in the actual cases decided.

▶ 2 ◀ PROBLEMS AND PROPOSITIONS

The morning newspaper and the weekly press abound with stories of advocates seeking to influence the belief and action of others on propositions of public policy: Msgr. George W. Casey of the Boston archdiocese expresses his concern over the financial ability of the Roman Catholic Church to support parochial education and advocates shutting down Catholic grade schools. California Superintendent of Public Instruction Maxwell Rafferty voices fears about the lack of "patriotism" in public school curricula and proposes that teachers "indoctrinate" their students "to revere the great Americans of the past, to cherish traditions of our country, to hate communism and its creatures like hell. . . ."[1] Psychologist Albert Bandura verbalizes anxieties relating to the exposure of young people to television violence and concludes that such violence heightens aggressive tendencies in children.

The advocate seeks to influence others to accept his position on a matter of public belief or policy. This position represents his attitude toward whatever controversy is verbalized through a proposition. *A proposition is a conclusion about a controversy*, a conclusion believed by the advocate and a conclusion the advocate wishes to persuade others to accept. It grows out of and reflects concern and anxiety toward an accepted belief or behavioral pattern, which is often called the *status quo*.

Whatever the proposition, whether it urges the indoctrination of students in public schools or the abandonment of church responsibility for elementary education, it is associated with a real or imagined threat of people's needs, values, or purposes. Such a threat can assume two roles. The present state of affairs, if continued, can prevent the fulfillment of needs, values, and purposes. (If television violence is not curbed, the aggressive tendencies of the growing generation will present serious social consequences.) Or the present state of affairs may itself be threatened by the acceptance of certain belief and action. (If students are not indoctrinated with anti-Communist patriotism, the nation may turn to Communism.)

All propositions express controversies which have originated in anxiety and which have grown out of personal and group insecurities, fears, and dissatisfactions. Such anxieties occur when individuals feel they are unable to tolerate given beliefs and actions; they have reason to believe that the continuance of a situation will result in injurious effects. Propositions, therefore, state complaints stemming from anxieties, and inherent to the statement of complaint in any proposition is the advocate's solution to that complaint in the form of expressed or implied proposed changes which will, if accepted, relieve or remove altogether the original anxieties. Even though Dr. Bandura does not specify a solution in his proposition on television violence, the implied proposition suggests that young people should have minimal exposure to such violence. Such a proposal both reflects a controversy (the television industry disclaims correlation between viewing violence and performing violence; various psychologists have asserted a sizable degree of correlation), and initiates further controversy.

A proposition, then, represents potential or actual conflict of opinion and fact. It channels anxieties into a form or mold which facilitates and permits rational deliberation preparatory to democratic resolution of a controversy. Anxieties over alleged conspiracies which seem to threaten the traditional American way of life are channeled into the proposition "the traditional American way of life is being betrayed from within by a Communist conspiracy"—a proposition probably implied in the attacks of certain "patriotic" organizations on public education. Insecurities created by the "separate but equal" doctrine of *Plessy v. Ferguson* resulted in long agitation on the part of many groups of Americans for a reversal of that holding, their anxieties being channeled into a proposition calling for a different interpretation of the Fourteenth Amendment. Fears that the structural linguists would undermine the whole idea of authority or correctness in language led to the proposal that the third edition of *Webster's New International Dictionary* (unabridged) should be rejected in favor of the second edition. And anxieties relating to its possible effect on the moral behavior of high school students have brought about proposals that the *Dictionary of American Slang* should be removed from school libraries.

In each of these cases insecurities and anxieties concerning the ability of the *status quo* to deal effectively with problems, or the survival of the *status quo* itself, led to lack of toleration. That intolerance found expression in a conclusion-complaint, the proposition.

Every proposition possesses a background or history all its own; the proposition did not suddenly happen; it emerged from a complex process of controversy evolution. From the inception of a situation which created basic original concerns to the focusing of those concerns through the proposition, this evolutionary development demands the study of the advocate. The advocate must be aware of the evolution, for without the perception and knowledge such a study results in, he would work in an atmosphere of relative ignorance. He could be compared to the theatre-goer who arrives at the beginning of the last act of a fashionable play, unable to pass judgment on the act or the play because of his unawareness of the plot. The evolution of a proposition represents the "plot" for the advocate; his advocacy is only the climax or the final act. Unfortunately, in society there are too many "last-act advocates" who attempt to carry out their responsibilities partially or largely unaware of the "plot" of the proposition they defend. They see only the end product, not the processes; they see only the flower, not the root.

EVOLUTION OF A PROPOSITION

There are, at any given time in free society, literally thousands of problems of public concern, each one possessing the potential threat to disturb the security of large numbers of citizens sufficiently to create wholesale public opinion, hence public controversy, on the problem. W. Phillips Davison of the Rand corporation expressed the potential in this way:

The analogy of seeds illustrates the growth of ideas. Seeds in thousands are scattered over the landscape. Some fall on rocks and fail to germinate. Others take root and die because they lack soil in sufficient depth or because they are smothered by faster growing weeds. Only a few fall on earth when the conditions are right for continuated growth and multiplication.

Similarly, there are many more issues that might provide the basis for mass movements than ever see the light of day. All men have grievances, inspirations, and ideas . . . but most of these die away in mutterings or casual conversations. An issue begins to take root only when it is communicated from one person to a second, who then carries it further in his own conversation. Most potential issues disappear from attention before this human chain grows to appreciable length, but the few that survive form the basis for public opinion.[2]

In San Francisco in the spring of 1963, large numbers of citizens, with apparent suddenness, decided that the city was in the midst of a crime wave of monumental importance. They demanded that some sort of action be taken. The expression of these anxieties was to become a primary public issue in the city elections that year, and that public issue was, in effect, a proposition—a conclusion about a controversy. What was the genesis of the proposition?

One evening, as a nurse from a large city hospital waited for a bus, an unknown man attempted to assault her. On the same night two other ladies, walking from a bus-stop to their homes, were held up and robbed. Two hours later the owner of a grocery store was robbed and beaten by a masked assailant. At the same time, in another part of the city, a bus driver was severely beaten by a "gang of young people." These four events in one evening, it is suggested, were not uncommon to San Francisco, or to any major city of a million people. Yet they resulted in the development of a proposition of significant public controversy.

All of the victims recounted their stories to the police, of course, and investigations were begun. Inherent to all of the complaints were assertions of causation; that is, reasons *why* each had been victimized. Each victim complained about the lack of police protection throughout the city, expressing both fears concerning his own future safety and concern over the safety and well-being of the whole metropolitan community. Their assertions were not just confined to police reports. The following morning both morning newspapers reported the incidents in brief stories on the inside pages without judgment as to possible causes. And the victims communicated the incidents, along with their own conclusions, to members of their primary groups —friends, relatives, and associates. As communication took place members of the primary groups began placing the incidents within the context of their own experiences and anxieties. Perhaps they remembered speeding cars driven by "irresponsible teen-agers"; possibly they recalled being "followed" by "suspicious-looking people" down a dark street late at night; maybe they recalled a relative or friend losing a purse or a package to a downtown thief, or a night on the streetcar when "young thugs" threatened the motor-man.

As members of the primary groups passed on information relating to the criminal acts, they incorporated into their communication their own perceptions not only of what had taken place, but of what might take place in the future if nothing were done. The assertion that the city "wasn't a safe place for decent people" began to be popularized, with the causal relationship, "because of lack of police protection," more and more frequently attached. Public opinion was beginning to form.

At this point of time when the seeds of public opinion could have been smothered by other pressing problems, some opinion leadership developed. Physicians at the hospital where the nurse was employed, men known not to make hasty judgments, protested both to the police and the city government. Businessmen friends of the grocer, reputable members of the community, alerted other businessmen to the problem. The minister of the church the two ladies attended brought the problem to the attention of his congregation. The president of the local union the bus driver belonged to publicly warned the city his union would not tolerate a situation in which the lives of union members were jeopardized. As we observed in the previous chapter, public opinion represents the generalized judgment of a *considerable* number of people on a matter of public concern. These opinion leaders undoubtedly brought the problem to the attention of considerable numbers.

The next step in the evolution of a proposition involved the context within which the problem of police protection was to function. Recall that 1963 was an election year in the city; a new mayor was to be chosen. There were at least five candidates for mayor, each seeking conclusions on public problems to present to the electorate. One of the candidates was immediately concerned by the reaction of the opinion leaders. (The others may also have been concerned but did not express themselves at this time.) Not only was this candidate concerned, but he recognized in the situation what he felt to be an excellent campaign issue, one on which the public could be aroused, as well as an issue on which his position might create a favorable image of himself as a "future mayor." In his analysis he associated the crimes and their resulting concern with inadequate law enforcement, and inadequate law enforcement was but a part of the syndrome pointing clearly to the lack of sensitivity on the part of the city government, the "in-group," to the needs of the citizens.

In a public address a few nights later this candidate spoke of "the callous crime of neglect, the unwillingness of the city administration to provide the people of this city with the security of life and property they need and demand." He referred to three of the four cases previously cited, in addition to several other recent cases of violence committed against citizens. The address was carried on television.

The speech of the candidate symbolized a new and vital leadership, one not associated with the primary group (as the previous opinion leaders had been). The candidate, as a leader, was able to communicate to far greater numbers of people, and, at the same time, was able to put public anxieties in some sort of context, the attitude of the city government.

In describing the evolutionary process so far we have not meant to suggest that all propositions have their origin in similar situations. This genesis appears to be the most common, but there are others. In some areas, such as science, a proposition may represent a controversy which emerged from independent or simultaneous discoveries. In philosophy a proposition may grow out of the development of an idea, that is, for every idea there is a counter idea. In behavioral science a proposition may emerge from a prediction as to human behavior. Propositions may grow out of human instinct for change, out of the evolution of man's social institutions or the desire for betterment. But whatever the origin, the pattern of development is similar: a small group is aroused by a threat, and that group becomes, as Paul Lasswell puts it, a "radiating nucleus for an idea." In short, the threat, translated into a problem, finds human groupings hospitable to it. From these groupings some kind of leadership emerges, a leadership which is responsible for the development of initial public opinion. If the leadership fails to function, if public opinion fails to germinate, the problem is, at least temporarily, forgotten.[3]

The San Francisco press, which had originally given matter-of-fact and limited coverage of the four incidents of crime, now became motivated by the political leadership which had emerged. The press could no longer treat the problem cursorily, for the primary group problem had now become a more extensive public problem associated with the basic proposition concerning what person should be mayor during the next four years. Therefore, the press, the day after the television speech on city crime, gave the problem both thorough and opinionated coverage. One newspaper took the position that charges of "inadequate law enforcement" were exaggerated and absurd and that the crime rate in San Francisco was comparable to that of any major city. Two other newspapers took opposite positions, both verifying the charges and demanding reforms. One paper even went so far as to suggest the possible presence of a crime syndicate in the city.

At this juncture, then, the press assumed a leadership role of its own in arousing and directing public opinion. At the same time the press, by taking opposing points of view, made the problem one of open public controversy, an important function as we have heretofore seen. Not only was the newspaper press becoming involved with the problem, but also the radio and television press began to give coverage. Thus the mass media informed additional large numbers of people, formulating the problem in such a manner that it was understandable and interesting. The press directed attention to a problem; it stimulated interest and a curiosity to know more about the problem; it attempted to direct opinion into action or, at least, a readiness for action. After several days of exposure to mass media discussion of crime and law enforcement, considerable numbers of San Franciscans were aroused not only by acts of violence, but also by the suggestion that these acts were made possible by an apathetic city administration.

One must not assume that *most* of the citizens were aroused. Perhaps not even a majority were very concerned, even though a majority were by this time probably familiar with the problem. Moreover, one should not assume that, of those aroused, the majority favored a change in the *status quo*. That remained to be seen. The important fact is that a substantial number of citizens *were* concerned after the mass media broadly publicized the problem and that their concern was sufficient to sustain the momentum of the evolution.[4]

Through mass media the original anxieties and the concerns of the primary groups and opinion leaders were transformed into a problem potentially affecting an entire community. At this point face-to-face discussion began once more, discussion resembling the original primary group deliberations but now proceeding with the understanding of those concerned that large numbers of people in the community were involved with the same problem. The problem, therefore, had different connotations and meanings from the original anxieties discussed previously by the primary groups. The problem was now more significant and had deeper implications in that it was associated with a larger proposition concerning the broad policy a city administration should follow. A circular process was thus established; the more public discussion that took place, the more public communication resulting from discussion; the more public communication engaged in, the more concern which in turn led to more discussion, and so on.

Sometime during this phase the majority of citizens entered the process, acquiring some knowledge on the problem and forming at least tentative conclusions about it. Members of the Commonwealth Club listened to two candidates for mayor describe their reactions to the problem; a church congregation heard the chief of police take the position that the public was becoming hysterical over a situation that was not serious at all. Discussion at a cocktail hour, an executives' meeting, a student rally brought the problem more closely to the attention of citizens. These exposures to communication allowed citizens to arrive at both individual and group attitudes on the problem, attitudes which varied from remote or casual to real concern. Communication also led to individual and group positions on the problem, from positions highly critical of the present state to positions which strongly defended the *status quo*. In short, public opinion did not develop in one direction. At least two different general opinions evolved, and the clash of these two opinions meant controversy and the resolution of that controversy through advocacy.

On one side of the controversy, the side which upheld the position that there was no serious crime wave and that police protection was generally adequate, were the city administration, the police department, one daily newspaper, one candidate for mayor, and citizens who agreed with their position. On the other side of the controversy, the side which upheld the position that crime was a serious and threatening problem and that the city administration, including the police department, seemed unwilling or unable to solve the problem, were various civic and religious groups, two daily newspapers, four candidates for mayor, and citizens who agreed with their position. Importantly enough, the public was aroused sufficiently to insist, through public opinion, on full-scale public debate.

At this juncture, spokesmen for the two sides began to formulate propositions which would permit public advocacy on the problem. Such propositions needed to channel the anxieties felt by the public into conclusions which allowed and promoted rational deliberation. The propositions should have expressed complaints and set forth alternatives to the *status quo* which would have permitted advocates representing opposing viewpoints to communicate their positions and the reasons for those positions to the public.

The general proposition that developed could be stated something like the following: "Inadequate police protection in the city of San Francisco has resulted in serious dangers to the life and property of the people of the city." The various spokesmen, however, did not always phrase their propositions in this way. They employed conclusions which appeared to express only a phase of the general proposition: "We must add 400 policemen to the force and sanction the use of police dogs where they would be effective." "The problem is in part the fault of inadequate street lighting; we should double the number of street lights." "The only sound approach is to attack the conditions in this city that produce crime and to improve our facilities and methods of dealing with delinquents so they won't become criminals." Each conclusion actually dealt only with a proposal for solving a problem these spokesmen "assumed" existed.

Spokesmen against the general proposition, those who rejected the conclusion that there were serious dangers to life and property, on the other hand, confined their advocacy more closely to the general proposition, arguing that (1) the city crime rate was not unreasonable; (2) mass hysteria had distorted reality; (3) the city police department was among the finest in the country; (4) the citizens, therefore, were among the best protected citizens in the nation. They avoided argument over the various solutions, probably feeling such argument unnecessary.

Public advocacy in the form of public debate represented the final phase of the evolution of a proposition. Once the advocates had completed their task of attempting to persuade the public to their positions, the public registered a final verdict on the proposition through the ballot. Public opinion on this proposition then dissolved, and the public moved its attention to other anxieties and other problems.

The following steps have been observed in the evolution of a public proposition:

1. Individual concern and anxiety over a threat to security (attacks on nurse, bus driver, grocer, etc.)
2. Relation of threat to a problem; attachment of causation (inadequate police protection; indifference)
3. Communication of problem to primary groups (friends, relatives, associates)
4. Communication by primary groups to others beyond the groups; development of opinion leaders (influential citizens become involved)
5. Assumption of leadership by persons not in primary groups (candidate for mayor)
6. Arousal of public opinion by the mass media (stimulation of interest; direction of opinion; attachment of problem to broader issues)
7. Resumption of face-to-face discussion in multiple groups of original problem placed in larger context (circular process)
8. Formulation of individual and group attitudes and positions (through exposure to knowledge, discussion, and group sampling)
9. Channeling of problem and alternatives into a proposition (spokesmen formulate propositions expressing concern and complaint)
10. Public debate on the proposition by advocates; resolutions of problem; dissolution of public opinion.

An essentially similar process may be observed in the evolution of almost all public controversies. The involved group, of course, changes. The group may be composed of citizens of a community, a state, a section of the country, a nation, or a group of nations. The group may cut across geographic lines and consist of teen-agers, senior citizens, attorneys, educators, employees, union members, believers in a particular religion, Democrats, Republicans, socialists, or various combinations thereof. Whatever the group and its composition, there are "seeds of concern and threat" that fall among it, and some of these seeds take root and become problems and eventually propositions. Believers in the cult of correctness experience a threat from the structural linguists and eventually propose that a dictionary is "barbaric"; advocates for states' rights witness fears related to Federal power and propose amendments to the Constitution; educational philosophers feel concern over an educational system geared to pragmatism and demand a different philosophic undergirding; a medical association finds itself unable to tolerate anxieties toward a proposed Federal medical care program and works for its defeat. In each case anxieties are symbolized in problems; causes are identified; communication creates leadership; mass media arouse the particular group concerned; problems are formulated into propositions; advocacy resolves the controversy.

MAKING THE PROPOSITION FUNCTIONAL

We observed the difficulties advocates attacking police protection in San Francisco had in formulating a proper and effective proposition which would facilitate rational deliberation on the real problem experienced by a sizable number of citizens. Not one adequately phrased a proposition which facilitated debate on the major implications and issues of the problem. As a result, the issue concerning whether or not a serious and threatening situation actually existed was virtually ignored. Similarly ignored was the matter of causation; if serious problems were proven to exist, then what were their causes? Perhaps the cause was inadequate police protection; perhaps the cause was something else, or maybe there were multiple causes. These candidates concentrated on solutions to problems they had not established as existing. They discussed and advocated more policemen, the use of police dogs, better street lighting, and improved guidance programs for juvenile offenders. Solutions demanded debate, of course, but so did the existence of threats and their causes. What was needed, and what was apparently most difficult to find, was a proposition which would reflect the essential points of controversy and which would focus on the differing important points of view.

The difficulty was not unique. A great deal of advocacy takes place in the absence of an adequate proposition, and advocacy under such cicumstances is usually superficial and unrewarding. It has to be unrewarding, for unless a proposition is able to produce controversy on *all* of the essential issues involved, a public cannot very well render a wise decision. The problem of devising such a proposition is the problem of *making a proposition functional,* channeling the anxieties and the basic points of controversy into an encompassing conclusion which an audience is asked to accept or reject.

Propositions can be verbalized in many ways: as motions in clubs and small groups ("I move that. . . ."); as assertions or conclusions in informal situations ("I believe. . . ." "I think we should stop giving aid to dictators."); as resolutions in school debate ("Resolved, that. . . ."); as bills in legislative bodies ("Be it enacted that. . . ." or "A proposal to. . . ."); as indictments in criminal law or complaints in civil action ("The grand jury charges. . . ." or "Therefore plaintiff demands. . . ."). Of considerable importance in the verbalization of any proposition is a simple fact—the quality and effectiveness of the advocacy that follows is directly affected by the statement of the proposition itself. Unless a proposition is made functional the debate concerning it may very well fail to address itself to the real problems giving rise to the proposition and the issues inherent to the proposition.

Making a proposition functional is an essential task of the advocate. (It should be pointed out that in some cases, because of commitments of a professional nature or because of the very close proximity of the advocate to issues or to friends involved in issues, the advocate does not have the choice of formulating a proposition. An attorney's proposition is already specified when he undertakes the defense of a person accused of automobile negligence; a worker for Boeing may have little choice but to defend the proposition that a Boeing-built experimental aircraft would be superior to one built by General Dynamics, etc.) In this essential task the advocate must, first of all, make a distinction as to the eventual purpose of the advocacy as it relates to a given proposition.

There are two primary purposes: *Non-policy-making advocacy* has as its purpose the arousal and development of public opinion on a proposition of public policy. The general advocate attempts to influence as many people as he can to accept his position on a proposition. His efforts are directed at affecting public policy through public opinion. *Policy-making advocacy* has as its purpose to directly influence public policy. The special advocate speaks in front of those who will pass judgment on a proposition; he engages in public debate for the purpose of influencing those who make policy decisions.

The general advocate speaks at a political rally, at a luncheon club, in front of his classmates, at an informal get-together of friends. He uses advocacy in the attempt to affect the belief and/or action of his particular audience, knowing that if he is successful, they will probably go on to influence others in the same direction. Eventually, he hopes, public opinion will be directed in part through his advocacy and will, in the end, exert pressure sufficient to bring about the change he advocates.

The special advocate is normally involved in formalized debate. A congressman has ten minutes to demonstrate his position on a bill and, at the same time, attack arguments against his position. An attorney prepares and presents a case in behalf of his client and defends that case after it is attacked by an opposing attorney. A school debater presents both a constructive speech and a rebuttal, in both clashing his opinions against those of his opponent. In all of these situations the advocate seeks a directed formal decision on the merits of his case. When the debate is over, a vote will be taken and a decision reached.

Knowing the purpose of the advocacy helps the advocate to determine the requirements for making a proposition functional.

Problems of phrasing a proposition to be used in general advocacy make relatively few demands. Since it is not directly associated with life and property, that is, it does not demand an immediate decision by a policy-making group, oftentimes the proposition need not be stated explicitly at all. A change in belief or a course of action may be suggested. A speaker at a public meeting may review the needs for Congressional reform; he may even spell out the reforms he thinks prudent (an end to the seniority system, easier methods of bringing about closure), but he need not incorporate these into a formalized proposition. His proposition is understood.

Whether or not the proposition is formally stated in general advocacy, however, the advocate ought to make perfectly clear the nature of the problem he is concerned with. This should come both in the introduction to his address and in the development of the nature and seriousness of the problem in the body of the address.

If the advocate does spell out a proposition, the proposition should allow him to focus on the basic issues involved, i.e., the essential points of disagreement between his position on the proposition and that of an opponent, who may or may not present his position at the same occasion. The proposition should epitomize the threats and anxieties which resulted in the conceptualization of those threats through the proposition. It should indicate clearly the attitude of the advocate toward the proposition, that is, his position on the conclusion. And the proposition should indicate the desired audience reaction, that specific behavior the advocate expects from his audience as a result of his address.

A proposition for general advocacy exists so that the advocate may thoroughly explore a public problem for the benefit of an audience. (The advocate often hopes to persuade an audience by educating that audience.) Thorough exploration results in two items: (1) significant questions relating to the resolution of the proposition are deliberated, and (2) extraneous or insignificant questions are ignored or put into proper perspective. Consider two cases in point in which public advocacy was quite futile because these two factors did not function.

Recently, rightist groups have launched what amounts to a concerted and nation-wide attack on public education. Their general proposition is difficult for the observer to state and seemingly impossible for them to state themselves. But it is probably similar to the following: Contemporary public education is failing to preserve the "American way of life." The proposition is a thoroughly legitimate one, and one worthy of public advocacy. Through its deliberation advocates *could* address themselves to both the strengths and shortcomings of American education, the goals and purposes of education, and reasons why those purposes were not being met, if they weren't. Solutions *could* be proposed and debated. In short, advocacy growing out of such a proposition could make a real contribution to the improvement of public education in America. Unfortunately, such a proposition has not been functionalized by rightist advocates, either in written or spoken advocacy. As a result, rather than debating the real issues in education—financing, teacher training, and curriculum—these advocates have concerned themselves with pseudo-propositions, propositions which avoid vital issues, which do not channel significant problems into a form which permits rational deliberation. In public meetings, rightist advocates deliberate over the censorship of textbooks, the indoctrination of students, what is to be done about teachers and administrators who are "soft on subversives," and how to make schools more patriotic. A functional proposition might not be the whole answer, but such a proposition might help a great deal in getting such advocates to focus their attention on the basic issues* in American public education.

Take another case in point. A Midwestern community recently involved itself in a controversy concerning its high school library. Responding to the complaints of several students that they were unable to prepare term papers because the library was "inadequate," public opinion in the community concerned itself with the adequacy of the library. The "propositions" emerging from public opinion, however, did not adequately reflect the real problems or issues in controversy. The PTA argued simply that the library did not have "enough books." A civic club argued over whether or not the library included the "right kind of books." The school administration developed the proposition that the library was insufficiently staffed. The board of education argued that if students would stop stealing books, the library would be acceptable. A local patriotic organization laid the trouble to "Communist influence" and questioned the loyalty of the librarian who had asked previously for books the organization regarded as "subversive." The librarian complained of lack of funds. The quarreling factions were unable to agree on a single, encompassing, controversial conclusion. A full and productively rewarding debate was thus precluded. A functional proposition, such as the following might have aided in promoting helpful advocacy: "The high school library is inadequate for the needs of the high school students." Using this proposition the specific needs of the students could have been rationally examined, and those needs could then have been contrasted with available material and services. Under the canopy of this proposition dissident groups could also have deliberated the problems of the "right kind of books," "book stealing," "Communist influence," and "lack of funds," all of these opinions being put into proper priority of concern in the process.

These are some of the problems faced by the general advocate, in both formal and informal situations, in attempting to make any proposition functional. The criteria discussed are equally applicable to the advocate who engages in public debate. He, too, must work with a proposition which channels anxieties, problems, and issues into a mold which facilitates rational deliberation. His proposition must also indicate a desired audience reaction, and his position on the proposition must be made quite clear.

CLASSIFYING THE PROPOSITION

Propositions for advocacy may be classified according to function solely in terms of the behavioral response the affirmative advocate seeks from his audience. The purpose of classification is that of better enabling the advocate to prepare an analysis of the proposition so that its requirements for proof can be determined. Saying this does not mean, however, that once a proposition has been classified the advocate automatically has a pattern of analysis in front of him. Analysis is a far more complex and time-consuming process than that, as we shall observe in the next chapter. Classification does suggest, however, approaches to the determination of the issues inherent within a given proposition. In terms of the behavioral response desired by an affirmative, propositions can be divided into those of *belief* and those of *action*.

Propositions of Belief ask the acceptance of conclusions of fact and value; they seek not an overt response from an audience, but an intellectual-emotional assent to a conclusion. An audience is asked to agree to a fact, idea, set of circumstances, theory, belief, event, or relationship alleged to exist. Often such propositions ask merely for a factual judgment: A jury is asked to believe the fact that X is guilty of embezzlement, or Y committed an act of automobile negligence. More often such propositions ask the audience to resolve the controversy of the proposition through the expression of a value judgment concerning the goodness or badness, rightness or wrongness, desirability or undesirability of an idea, situation, person, event, or institution. An audience may be asked to pass judgment on whether or not force is the most effective weapon of implementing social change. An audience may be asked to believe that science should supply the bases of the assumptions of modern ethics and culture. An audience may be asked to decide whether or not the Court decision on nonsectarian prayer was good or bad, desirable or undesirable. In each case, before the audience can formally express its belief on the proposition, it must examine its own values—social, political, cultural, religious, and so forth—and relate the findings of that examination to the specific conclusion the advocate draws. Values are concepts of socially acceptable behavior, "yardsticks" by which individuals and groups compare what they need to do or are asked to do with what is, at a given time, socially acceptable to do. One could not reach a personal decision on the goodness or badness of the non-sectarian prayer decision until he had weighed that decision in terms of such political values as freedom of speech, equality of opportunity, and the importance of the individual, as well as such religious values as the importance of religious education and the separation of church and state.

Propositions of Action concern themselves with the acceptance or rejection of a conclusion calling for overt behavior, not merely an emotional-intellectual assent: X should serve three years in prison for embezzlement; the President's tax legislation should be enacted; the Court decision on prayer should be reversed; the Roman Catholic Church should close its elementary schools; the study of science should be a curricular requirement during all twelve years of public school; anti-Communist courses should be taught in high schools. The advocate upholding a proposition of action seeks agreement on a course of action or a commitment to action. "Action," wrote John Dewey, "is the means by which a problematic situation is resolved . . . the settling of future conditions under which a life process goes on."[5]

The reader must understand the close relationship between propositions of belief and action. As a rule, belief represents readiness for action, and almost always, except in irrational situations, action is based on belief. The advocate must pass through propositions of belief so that he may reach propositions of action. No man may be sentenced to prison (a proposition of action) unless he is first judged guilty of some act (a proposition of belief). It is the jury's role to determine guilt in most cases (belief), and the judge's responsibility to sentence (action). Similarly, the advocate must deal with propositions of belief relating to the desirability or undesirability of basing a culture, or the ethics of that culture, on the assumptions of science before he seeks the acceptance of a proposition calling for educational curricular changes which would emphasize the predominant role of science. A proposition of action demanding passage of a constitutional amendment which would change the amending process is actually the outgrowth of propositions of belief concerning the goodness, rightness, and judiciousness of the growth of Federal power. Such propositions, and the values they represent, must be resolved by an audience before that audience consents to action.

► N O T E S ◄

1. As quoted in "Hate Campaign," *Look Magazine* (October 22, 1963), p. 56.
2. W. Phillips Davison, "The Public Opinion Process," *Public Opinion Quarterly* (Summer, 1958), p. 93.
3. See Davison, *ibid.;* Elihu Katz and Paul F. Lazarsfeld, *Personal Influence: The Part Played by People in the Flow of Communication* (New York: The Free Press of Glencoe, 1955); William Albright, "Two Decades of Opinion Study," *Public Opinion Quarterly* (Spring, 1957), pp. 14-23; Floyd Allport, "Toward a Science of Public Opinion," *Public Opinion Quarterly* (January, 1937), pp. 7-23; Richard LaPiere, *Theory of Social Control* (New York: McGraw-Hill Book Company, 1954).
4. See Wilbur Schramm, *The Processes and Effects of Mass Communication* (Urbana, Ill.: The University of Illinois Press, 1954); Frederick C. Ivion, *Public Opinion and Propaganda* (New York: Thomas Y. Crowell Company, 1952); Joseph T. Klapper, *The Effects of Mass Communication* (New York: The Free Press of Glencoe, 1960).
5. John Dewey, *The Quest for Certainty* (New York: G. P. Putnam's Sons, 1929), pp. 244-245.

► E X E R C I S E S ◄

1. What difficulties would advocates have in attempting to argue the following propositions?

   a. Franklin D. Roosevelt was the greatest American president.
   b. Freudian psychoanalysis is entirely too negative.
   c. American policy toward the Soviet Union should be changed.

    d. *Tea and Sympathy* should not be produced by the local high school.

2. From the following "problem areas" formulate both a proposition of belief and one of action:

    a. The role of the radical right within a two-party structure based on moderation

    b. The relation between America's political structure and the complexities of twentieth century economic and social structures

    c. Congressional investigations and civil liberties

    d. Reapportionment of state legislatures and the Federal courts

    e. Television in free society

    f. Presidential succession

    g. Federal assistance to education

    h. The effectiveness of Congress

    i. Foreign Aid

    j. Chronic unemployment

Make sure that each proposition is properly phrased; that it provides equitable grounds for controversy; that it clearly states that which the affirmative wants; that it clearly places the obligation for proof on the affirmative.

3. Read several editorials and letters to the editor in recent newspapers and magazines. Determine the proposition the advocate is arguing in each editorial and letter. State the proposition so that an intelligent debate or series of speeches of advocacy could take place.

4. Read one of the following books. State the proposition supported by the writer and describe how he attempts to support the proposition. You may wish to investigate the origin of the proposition and its social or psychological evolution from problem to proposition.

    a. J. K. Galbraith, *American Capitalism: The Concept of Countervailing Power* (Boston: Houghton-Mifflin Company, 1952).

    b. Louis Hartz, *The Liberal Tradition in America* (New York: Harcourt, Brace & World, Inc., 1955).

c. W. W. Rostow, *The United States in the World Arena* (New York: Harper & Row, Publishers, 1960).

d. Daniel Bell, *The End of Ideology* (New York: The Free Press of Glencoe, 1960).

e. Eric Fromm, *Psychoanalysis and Religion* (New Haven: Yale University Press, 1950).

f. David Riesman, *The Lonely Crowd* (New York: Doubleday & Company, Inc., 1950).

g. C. Wright Mills, *The Power Elite* (New York: Oxford University Press, 1956).

h. Rolf Hochhuth, *The Deputy* (New York: The Grove Press, 1964).

i. Martin L. Gross, *The Brain Watchers* (New York: New American Library, 1962).

j. Ralph Lapp, *Kill and Overkill* (New York: Basic Books, Inc., 1962).

k. Albert Camus, *The Stranger* (New York: Alfred A. Knopf, Inc., 1946).

l. William Golding, *Lord of the Flies* (New York: G. P. Putnam's Sons, 1955).

m. Rachel Carson, *Silent Spring* (Boston: Houghton-Mifflin Company, 1962).

5. Chapter two discusses the social evolution of a proposition. Ten steps in this evolution are suggested—from individual concern and anxiety through public advocacy. For one or more of the following problem areas trace the evolution of the problem from origin to proposition of public advocacy. Some initial references for research are suggested. Attempt to discover why and how the problems evolved into vital advocacy.

a. The Nature of the American Union, 1830–1861:
Ernest J. Wrage and Barnet Baskerville, *American Forum* (New York: Harper & Row, Publishers, 1960), 117 ff.
Allan Nevins, *The Ordeal of the Union,* 2 vols., (New York: Charles Scribner's Sons, 1947).

b. The Debate over Imperialism, 1898–1903:
Walter Millis, *The Martial Spirit* (Boston: Houghton-Mifflin Company, 1931).

Julius W. Pratt, *Expansionists of 1898* (Baltimore: Johns Hopkins Press, 1936).

William L. Langer, *The Diplomacy of Imperialism* (New York: Alfred A. Knopf, Inc., 1951).

c. Modernism versus Fundamentalism in Religion:

Norman F. Furniss, *The Fundamentalist Controversy: 1918–1931* (New Haven: Yale University Press, 1954).

Gail Kennedy (ed.), *Evolution and Religion* (Boston: D. C. Heath, 1957).

d. Isolationism versus One World:

William L. Langer and S. Everett Gleason, *The Challenge to Isolationism, 1937–1940* (New York: Harper & Row, Publishers, 1952).

Walter Johnson, *The Battle Against Isolation* (Chicago: The University of Chicago Press, 1944).

Wayne S. Cole, *America First: The Battle Against Intervention* (Madison: The University of Wisconsin Press, 1953).

e. McCarthyism and the Communist Conspiracy:

Richard Rovere, *Senator Joe McCarthy* (New York: Harcourt, Brace & World, Inc., 1959).

William E. Buckley and L. Brent Bozell, *McCarthy and His Enemies* (Chicago: H. Regnery Co., 1954).

▶ 3 ◀ RATIONAL PROCESSES: EXPLORATION AND ANALYSIS

The natural tendency of man is to do something at once; there is impatience with suspense, and lust for immediate action. When action lacks means for control of external conditions, it takes the form of acts which are the prototypes of rite and cult. Intelligence signifies that direct action has become indirect. It continues to be overt, but it is directed into channels of examination and exploration of conditions and doings that are tentative and preparatory. Instead of rushing "to do something about it," action centers upon finding out something about obstacles and resources and upon projecting inchoate later modes of defining response. Thinking has been well called deferred action. . . . Deferred action is present exploratory action.

John Dewey[1]

The "natural tendency" of the advocate is to defend his proposition at once. This chapter proposes to discuss the vital processes of exploration and analysis that must be regarded as the *sine qua non* of responsible verbal confrontation, processes which, as Dewey phrased it, represent deterred action and an intelligence directed into channels of exploration. It is the underlying thesis of this chapter that effective advocacy cannot be engaged in prior to a thorough and responsible analysis of whatever proposition the advocate is charged with supporting or denying. To behave otherwise is to invite sophistry at best, demagoguery at worst.

ANALYSIS: A DEFINITION

Any one definition of analysis is apt to be inadequate, but the process known as analysis, nevertheless, must be identified. Any one methodology of analysis has limitations; consequently, methodology should probably be a distillation from many different sources. Analysis as a logical process is so vital to the success of advocacy that it deserves extended thought and treatment by every advocate. We shall discuss the question of methodology shortly, but in the meantime the problem of definition deserves attention.

The definition of analysis which seems best suited to the aims of the advocate is one posited by Rudolf Carnap, logical positivist, in his work *Philosophy and Logical Syntax:*

The function . . . is to analyze all knowledge, all assertions of science and everyday life in order to make clear the sense of each such assertion and the connections between them.

One of the principal tasks of the analysis of a given proposition is to find out the method of verification for that proposition. The question is: What reasons can there be to assert this proposition? or: How can we become certain as to its truth or falsehood? This question is called by the philosophers the epistemological question: epistemology, or the philosophical theory of knowledge, is nothing other than a special part of logical analysis, usually combined with some psychological questions concerning the process of knowing.[2]

The Carnapian definition concentrates on the question: "Through what means can this proposition be verified?" In doing so, it implicitly involves itself with many of the criteria of analysis suggested by other philosophers. Before one is equipped to say what is necessary for verification, he must have concerned himself with the orderly handling of things as Descartes taught; he must have made the obscure clear and located problems central to the proposition, as Kant suggested; he must have integrated relationships and groupings, historical flow and movement, as Hegel believed; he must have decided, as James asked, whether or not the proposition corresponded to the facts; and certainly he must have "found out what's the matter and what can be done about it" as Dewey admonished.

At the same time, the Carnapian definition allows the advocate to focus on his main responsibility, i.e., the proof of whatever proposition he is dealing with, and it reminds the advocate that proof cannot be sought until "requirements for proof" are verified through analysis. In short, through analysis the advocate seeks to determine what he must do in order to prove the validity of a proposition. The advocate who attempts the proof of his proposition without proper exploration and analysis is, as Descartes wrote, ". . . like a man who would attempt to spring at a bound from the base to the summit of a house, spurning the ladders provided for the ascent, nor not noticing them."[3]

ANALYSIS: THE METHODOLOGICAL QUESTION

There are several assumptions that should be made concerning analytic methodology.

A first assumption is that there is no one methodology which holds the secret of effective analysis. We can suggest a methodological framework and trust that it will meet many of the needs of the advocate as he copes with a proposition. But this framework should not be considered definitive, gilt-edged, or applicable to all situations. The advocate, in the final act, must find a methodology he is comfortable with, one which will do the job in the way he wants it done. This methodology can be arrived at only through slow, and perhaps painful, deliberation.

A second assumption is that analysis is a continuing process; it is not merely one phase of argumentation, it parallels all argument from the inception of the proposition to the end of advocacy on that proposition. There is a period of time in preparing for advocacy, of course, when the advocate devotes all of his time to analysis, but the fact that he does this does not imply there is no association between analysis and research, proposition formulation, use of materials of proof, structure of argument, attack and defense, and the other constituents of argumentation.

A third assumption is that analysis is one of the most difficult of all mental activities, particularly so in its initial phases. John Dewey recognized this when he warned that analysis often seemed like a "preliminary period of groping through a situation . . . characterized throughout by confusion."[4] Because of this fact, many advocates avoid all but superficial analysis; most are unwilling to stay very long with a process that of necessity must be slow, deliberate, and thorough. The good analyst is in no great hurry; he does not expect the "answers" through revelation, only through time, thought, and preparation. It takes time to transfer a dishevelled and murky problem into a tidy, cogent, and ordered analysis.

A fourth assumption concerns the state of mind of the advocate. It almost goes without saying that a closed mind, even though it goes through the motions of analysis, will never be an analytic mind. John Stuart Mill warned against the closed mind, the mind which was bound by obscurities, dogmas, emotions, and ignorance, and he beseeched his readers to defy absolutes. The advocate who approaches analysis as a process which will merely confirm his own preconceptions, biases, and dogmas is like the politician who began his speech by saying, "These are the conclusions on which I will base my facts." Analysis will not have served its truth-reality seeking purpose for that advocate. One must approach analysis with an open mind, with a feeling of Cartesian doubt about the whole of the proposition, ready to suspend judgment on the merits of the proposition and its issues, ready to move freely and thoroughly wherever the paths of truth seem to go, and certainly ready to admit, if necessary, that one's preconceptions concerning the proposition were partly or entirely wrong.

A fifth assumption is that analysis is a necessarily limited activity, limited through its own subjective qualities, limited through the experiences and involvements of the analyzer, and limited in that many of the highest forms of man's experiences seem beyond man's abilities to verbally analyze. In short, one need not expect, or even seek, absolute truth in analysis. One must constantly remind himself that whatever the end product of analysis, it will have its weaknesses and failures and that those failures are, indeed, the responsibility of the advocate.

With these assumptions entered, we may then answer the question: How does the advocate discover the method of verification for his proposition?

1 / A Study of the Proposition in Terms of Its Language and Meaning

Every incisive analysis begins with a study of the wording and meaning of the subject being considered. The advocate undertakes the proof, or disproof, of a proposition; his first task is that of understanding the meaning of his proposition. The philosopher Wittgenstein regarded this act as the most significant in analysis.[5] It is the job of the advocate to examine carefully and thoughtfully each term in the proposition both in relationship to itself (background, possible meanings, probable meaning in this situation, function, emotional responses, etc.), and in relationship to the other terms of the proposition (collective meaning of the words). Additionally, the advocate must examine the meaning of words individually and words collectively in relationship to both the user of the words (a possible opposing advocate) and the hearer of the words (an audience). What connotations and associations will they attach to the words, and will these be similar to those of the advocate?

The attorney charged with defending X on an indictment of embezzlement would assuredly first of all examine the exact nature of the charges against his client in order to determine as precisely as possible the meaning of the state statute on embezzlement. This meaning could then be applied to X's alleged misconduct. The advocate urging that Congress be given the power to reverse decisions of the Supreme Court would be particularly concerned with the phrase "power to reverse" and its meaning. In this case, he would have to relate that phrase to the understanding of those who formulated the proposition. This he could do through inference: Congress already has the power to reverse decisions of the Court in all but constitutional cases; therefore, the framer of the proposition must have had in mind "power to reverse" constitutional holdings.

The advocate demanding the reversal of the Supreme Court's decision on non-sectarian prayer would face the necessity of clearly defining the meaning of individual words: "reversal," "Supreme Court," "decision," "non-sectarian," and "prayer." Quite readily the reader can see the difficulty in obtaining agreement on the meaning of the word "reversal" alone, not to mention the other terms. Yet if argument is to proceed on the main proposition, some sort of understanding, if only a working agreement, must be reached. Once individual words are given meaning, the advocate considers words collectively. "Non-sectarian prayer" would be such a collection. Do the two words "mean" something different when juxtaposed? What emotional responses might the combination arouse in both advocate and audience? Finally, of course, the advocate would have to consider the meaning of the proposition as a whole. When all of the meanings are put together, what do they mean?

Propositions of belief would appear to offer particularly distressing problems of language and meaning. The advocate arguing that existentialism is a more desirable rationale for education than pragmatism faces not only the task of distilling meaning from quasi-unemotional terms, such as "existentialism" and "pragmatism," but has the very difficult task of attaching meaning to emotional and value-laden words, such as "more desirable" and "rationale." The search for meaning here may be long and laborious, but it, too, must be done.

The advocate supporting the proposition: "A scientific culture, rather than the traditional literary culture, should supply the knowledge and ethics for an age committed to rational truth and material practicability" (the proposition recently advocated by English critic and writer, C. P. Snow) would face problems of consensus and understanding on such terms as: "scientific culture," "traditional literary culture," "knowledge and ethics," and an "age committed to. . . ."

Fortunately, or unfortunately, there are no hard-and-fast rules which, when applied, resolve the problems of meaning and understanding. Each word, and combination of words, presents its own problems. What the advocate hopes to do is, through thought and study, formulate meanings which will accurately convey to both opponent and auditors what the advocate *means* when he uses a word or series of words. This meaning needs to be one generally acceptable to listeners and readers; accordingly, it must be fairly and honestly arrived at. The meaning may be a tentative one, a working definition, which both parties to a controversy agree shall be *the* meaning until and unless another meaning is arrived at. Generally speaking, the advocate should formulate his meanings so that argument over meaning is avoided. However, one must be quick to realize that in many propositions, especially those of belief, the central argument may well have to be over the meaning of terms.

2 / The Preparation of a Preliminary Question Memorandum

From the initial phase of analysis, the study of language and meaning, the second phase evolves naturally and easily. It is inevitable that in the consideration of each word meaning, numerous questions should be asked by the advocate. These questions not only say a great deal about the term they are associated with, they say a great deal about the proposition as a whole and offer valuable clues concerning the requirements for proof of that proposition. An illustration should help to explain what is meant here.

Assume yourself to be an advocate defending the proposition: "Force is the most effective weapon of implementing social change." As you face the task of establishing meaning for each word in the proposition, and combination of words, you discover yourself asking numerous questions. Concerning the term "force" you might ask the following series of questions: Is force the same as power? Is force the same as violence? Does force mean a *threat* to use power, or its actual use? What is the relationship of power to values? Is war the only form of force? Each question, in a very real sense, points the way to further exploration and examination. Each question demands additional research and study, since each is an "unknown" which must become known.

Concerning the term "social change" you might find yourself asking some of the following questions: What is the relationship between standard of living and social change? What is the relationship between individual dignity and social change? Again, each question suggests further exploration, and each raises subsidiary questions which must be answered before the main question can be answered.

The careful analyst compiles a memorandum based on his early investigation of the wording of the proposition. That memorandum constitutes a preliminary guide to both future research and analysis. Its constant expansion, quantitatively and qualitatively, suggests the process of analysis is well under way.

3 / Acquiring the Necessary Knowledge

It is axiomatic to say that the most responsible of advocates is the one who *knows* his proposition, who has, as Descartes put it, "arrived at a knowledge which takes in all things."[6] The acquisition of knowledge relating to a particular proposition is a vital step in the analytic process.

Bertrand Russell has written of the role knowledge plays in analysis. He writes of the great difficulty he often encounters in being able to analyze a subject sufficiently to write about it and how he meets the problem:

. . . when I wish to write . . . I must first soak myself in detail until all the separate parts of the subject matter are familiar. Then, someday, if I am fortunate, I perceive the whole, with all its parts duly interrelated. . . . The nearest analogy is first walking all over a mountain in a mist, until every path and ridge and valley is separately familiar, and then, from a distance, seeing the mountain whole and clear in bright sunshine.[7]

The initial question memorandum should in all cases be sufficient to motivate the advocate to research the proposition. From original research will come additional questions which cannot be answered without further research and study. Research continues until "every path and ridge and valley is separately familiar." Indeed, usually research is not discontinued until the proposition is resolved.

4 / Relating the Proposition to Its Milieu

As the philosopher G. W. F. Hegel reminds us, no proposition can be fully understood save as it is seen in its relations to everything else.[8] Once the advocate has an understanding of the meaning of the proposition; once he has acquired the necessary background of knowledge relating to the proposition, he must then relate the proposition to the broader issues which engulf it, placing it in its milieu or setting. This placing in perspective involves associating the proposition with its historical context, determining its genesis and following its evolution from anxiety to problem to proposition. It entails associating the proposition with whatever social, economic, political, and ethical problems or issues to which it might be indigenous. It means tracing influence, assigning motives, evaluating roles, establishing causality, determining symptoms and consequences, allocating responsibilities.

Consider this phase of analysis in terms of two propositions, one of action and one of belief. In 1953 and 1954 the United States Supreme Court heard arguments from opposing attorneys concerning the constitutionality of the famous Plessy doctrine (1896), which sanctioned separate but equal public facilities for the Negro race. The Plessy doctrine held that separate but equal facilities did not violate the equal protection clause of the Fourteenth Amendment (163 US 537). In 1953 a series of cases went to the Supreme Court from the states of Kansas, South Carolina, Virginia, and Delaware, all of them involving the same basic issue: Negro minors, through their legal representatives, were seeking the aid of the courts in obtaining admission to the public schools of their respective communities on a non-segregated basis. In short, the cases held that public school segregation *per se* violated the equal protection clause, hence was unconstitutional. All of the cases were to be determined by one decision of the Court, the case of *Brown v. Board of Education of Topeka, Kansas.* The plaintiffs in this case were Negro children of elementary school age who brought action in the U.S. District Court of Kansas to enjoin enforcement of a Kansas statute which permitted cities of more than 15,000 population to maintain separate school facilities for Negro and white students. Pursuant to that authority, the Topeka Board of Education elected to establish segregated elementary schools.

Assume for yourself the role of the advocates preparing a case to be argued before the Supreme Court on the proposition: "Since the separate but equal ruling of the *Plessy* case violates the equal protection clause of the Fourteenth Amendment, it should be overruled." Why would there be necessity to place the proposition in its milieu? How would you go about doing it? The first question almost answers itself. The *Brown v. Board of Education* proposition did not stand in isolation; rather, it was related to constitutional issues of vast significance, to historical trends and movements, to social-psychological theories, to political questions concerning the powers of the federal as opposed to the state governments, and to the numerous preceding cases on the same issues that had come before the courts. One could pursue argument only through analyzing the proposition by placing it in perspective.

How, then, would one have placed it in perspective? A first approach would be to study the proposition historically, the genesis and evolution of the problem of segregation in education. The first case concerning the problem was that of *Roberts v. City of Boston* in 1849, in which Charles Sumner asserted the right of a Negro girl to attend any school of her choice. From this case the advocate would move to a study of the Fourteenth Amendment, its purposes, its wording, its applications. The *Plessy v. Ferguson* case would be next, and it would demand thorough study and understanding. Then one would address himself to the many cases which took their precedent from *Plessy*: *Cumming v. Richmond County* (1899); *Berea College v. Kentucky* (1908); *Gong Lum v. Rice* (1927); *Murray v. Maryland* (1935); *Missouri* ex rel. *Gaines v. Canada* (1938); *Sipuel v. University of Oklahoma* (1946); *Sweatt v. Painter* (1950). In each case the advocate would be concerned with the issues brought before the Court, the cases presented by opposing advocates, evidence used, and the ruling of the Court, carefully noting strong and weak arguments, trends in development of argument, and bases on which decisions had been reached.

A second approach to relating the proposition to its environment would be to associate it with social-psychological, economic, political, and ethical issues. For instance, from a review of the *Sweatt* case, the advocate would have discovered that in this case issues of race status and inferiority were successfully argued for the first time. The attorneys offered testimony from anthropologists, psychologists, and educators to the effect that the Negro was as capable of learning as the white, that classification of students by race was arbitrary and unjust, and that segregation was harmful to the personality development of the Negro. Accordingly, they argued that no segregated Negro school could possibly provide equal educational opportunity. With these findings the advocate would begin a study in depth of the findings of sociology, psychology, education, etc., relating to the segregation of the races. He would study the effect of segregation itself on public education in terms of whether or not it could be proven that separation denoted the inferiority of the Negro group. Politically, the advocate might concern himself with the possible encroachments on rights reserved to the states and to the people in order to discover the relationship of the proposition to that political question. Economically, he might pursue the relationship between lack of equal educational opportunity and equal economic opportunity.

Once the proposition is thus placed in its setting, the advocate has a much clearer picture of the issues involved and the requirements of proof.

How are propositions of belief placed in their milieu? Consider the proposition that existentialism is a more desirable rationale for education than pragmatism. Clearly this proposition must be placed in the context of public and private education, as well as the two contending philosophies. Previous steps in analysis would not only have defined the terms in the proposition, but would have provided series of questions helpful in placing the proposition in perspective. The following question would invite study of America's public and private educational systems: What is the status of present-day education? Such a study would reveal both good and bad philosophies, methods, and results. From the beginning the advocate would then approach an understanding of pragmatism, its theses, implications, and the degree to which education in America has incorporated its beliefs. The writings of Pierce, James, and Dewey would be invaluable. The advocate would ask himself two questions: What would education based on pragmatic philosophy consist of? What would be the consequences of such education? The advocate might discover, for instance, that pragmatism as a practical, functional, empirical system seemed to meet America's needs and values in the past. Its emphasis on the scientific method, the spirit of inquiry, and so on made for industrial advancement and urbanization of society. As a creed extolling results and glorifying utility, it appears to have symbolized what Americans wanted taught in their schools. But what of the consequences of pragmatism? Professor Nancy Gayer suggested several educational consequences:

We now enjoy the fruit of pragmatism—the technological society. In spite of it, we are in a different mood; we no longer think progress inevitable; catastrophe is likely. Technology appears to be mastering us. Knowledge is running amuck, proliferating faster than we can contain it. And man has disappeared within the mass. He is anxiety-ridden and without the guide-lines of cherished values. He wonders whether science is enough. He will not renounce science. . . . But he would like to supplement his belief in science with something that will give him a comforting sense of identity and personal worth.[9]

From a study of pragmatism and its results the advocate would then move on to a similar study of existentialism, seeking answers to the same two questions: What would education based on existentialism consist of? What would be the consequences? Writings of such men as Jean Paul Sartre, Karl Jaspers, Martin Buber, Gabriel Marcel, Martin Heidegger, and Rollo May would be consulted and an understanding of existentialism gained. Such concepts as the radical contingency of man, the necessity for the individual to define his own values, personal responsibility and commitment, and the uniqueness of the individual would need to be explored. As for the educational consequences, the advocate might once again turn to the suggestions of Nancy Gayer:

> Existentialism offers mid-century man in his anguish new optimism and courage based on facing such hard facts of life as the certainty of death, one's essential aloneness, and an imagination-staggering uncaring universe . . . poses a new interpretation of truth, allowing man to believe or disbelieve in God as he chooses, without needing to come to grips with "rigorous logical proofs." It holds that valid solutions are to be found in man's emotions as much as in his cerebrations . . . reaffirms man's priority and importance as an existent and the desirability of his becoming an authentic person. It introduces to man the use and value of philosophizing as an everyday, do-it-yourself way of life. It posits a conception of history which tells man that it is up to him to save the world, or to destroy it.[10]

As the analysis continued, the analyzer would confront additional problems in associating the proposition with psychology, sociology, economics, and ethics, each problem demanding exploration for meaning and relationship.

5 / *Determining the Logical Requirements of Proof: Presumption, Burden of Proof, and Prima-facie Proof*

In any proposition there are logical relationships which determine the responsibilities of an affirmative or a negative advocate. These logical relationships are termed "presumption," "burden of proof," and *"prima-facie* proof," which may be translated into ordinary language as the position from which the conflict starts, the responsibility of proving a new position, and what must be done to logically establish the new position. An analysis of these relations within the proposition will indicate to the advocate where he stands and what he must prove. We will begin with the burden of proof and consider presumption later.

The *burden of proof* is the obligation resting with the complaining party in a controversy, the affirmative or the plaintiff, to establish by proof the reasons why the proposition should be accepted before being entitled to a reply from an opposing advocate, the negative or the defense. This burden rests on the side to a controversy which would lose the controversy if the complaint were rejected or if no progress at all were made toward its settlement, e.g., if in court the plaintiff failed to make an appearance. The burden of proof remains constant; it does not move from affirmative to negative. An advocate urging that all power to propose and ratify a constitutional amendment be given to state legislatures would have the burden of proof on that proposition, that is, it would be his responsibility as the complaining party to advance reasons for the adoption of his proposal before asking the opposing advocate to speak.

In order to discharge this burden of proof, an affirmative must present a *prima-facie* case, and that is a case rationally sufficient to support his proposition. Only through the proof of a *prima-facie* (or logically adequate) case can the affirmative position ultimately prevail. If a grand jury feels that an affirmative has failed to show reasons why a party should be indicted (a *prima-facie* case against the party), it will refuse to return an indictment. If the court feels that the prosecution has failed to present a *prima-facie* indictment in its opening statement in a trial, it will dismiss the complaint. Only when such a case has been presented and supported in any debate is there reason for an opposing advocate to reply to the charges and indictments.

In legislative debate a representative introducing a bill calling for an end to the Congressional seniority system, a system which gives committee chairmanships to members who have served longest in Congress, would have to demonstrate reasons why the system was injurious to the business of the Congress and hence to the welfare of the nation. He would also need to propose an alternative to the seniority system and prove that his alternative proposal would better take care of the business of the Congress. If he did these things, he would have presented a *prima-facie* case. In law, in order to establish the guilt of X, the prosecution must present an indictment of X through a *prima-facie* case. (The *status quo* in this case would presume X innocent until proved otherwise.) If X were charged with criminal embezzlement, such a case would attempt to establish the following contentions:

1. Certain property was misappropriated.
2. X misappropriated the property.
3. The misappropriation was fraudulent, i.e., without the consent of the owner.
4. The property was for the personal use of X.

The introduction and proof of these four contentions would constitute a *prima-facie* indictment of X, and his innocence would be temporarily suspended. It would then be the responsibility of the defense advocate to reestablish X's innocence through attacking the truth of one or more of the contentions. This responsibility is termed the "burden of reply" or the "burden of rebuttal." The burden of reply is the obligation of going forward in argument, imposed initially on the negative and thereafter on each party to the controversy after the other has presented his reply. It shifts constantly.

"Presumption" consists of the "advantage" which rests with that side in a controversy which would win if the complaint of the proposition were rejected or if no progress were made toward its settlement. Presumption is associated with attitudes represented by majority public opinion; it rests with the side that defends implicity or explicity, innocence, mores, customs, laws, tradition, possession, accepted beliefs, institutions, philosophies, and actions. This is not to say that presumption connotes any right or justice in the *status quo*, or even, for that matter, a tolerable state of affairs. Many advocates probably have a notion that because things have gone on a certain way, they are somehow good or desirable. That may indeed be so, but that is not what presumption means. Presumption simply states what exists. And because that which is, is so widely accepted, there is a certain advantage in defending its existence.

The affirmative, then, must suspend the advantage which rests with the *status quo*, and it does so through upholding its burden of proof.

A proposition should be worded so that the negative has the benefit of presumption. To argue that X is innocent of embezzlement as a proposition would throw presumption to the affirmative and the burden of proof to the negative. It would be strange indeed to hear a defense attorney arguing for his client's conviction. To debate a proposition suggesting that the United States should not provide medical care for its elderly citizens through social security funds, when in point of fact the United States currently *does not* follow this action, would similarly create a situation in which an affirmative, speaking or writing first, would be called upon to defend the *status quo* before it was attacked. The assumption is wisely and well founded that one need not be forced to defend the merits of current belief or action until they have been attacked.

It is important to note that the introduction and proof of a *prima-facie* case generally suspends the presumption only temporarily. Presumption may be restored by an opposing advocate's successful attack on the truth and validity of the arguments of an affirmative. Only the action of a jury or voting majority may permanently suspend presumption, for it is the responsibility of the voter, in the final analysis, to determine the fate of an alternative and the truth of a complaint. Only through that opinion is presumption suspended, restored, and removed. If in the opinion of the voter presumption has been maintained by the negative at debate's end, then that voter should decide to maintain the *status quo*.

There is frequently great difficulty in advocacy when a proposition introduced by an affirmative advocate is contested by a *counter-proposition* submitted by a negative advocate. The situation most frequently occurs in public debate.

A counter-proposition is the option of the advocate opposing the main proposition in any debate. If the opposing advocate wishes, he may admit in large measure the affirmative indictment or complaint (ordinarily that portion of the affirmative case which deals with the presence and seriousness of a problem), and, at the same time, disagree with the affirmative that the solution suggested by the proposition will satisfactorily deal with the problem both advocates admit to exist. In this case, particularly in propositions which call for specific action to be taken, the opposing advocate offers a solution of his own, which solution is not the continuance of the *status quo*. This solution is the counter-proposition, and the advocate who introduces it is saying in effect, "This proposal will solve problems both advocates admit need solving better than the proposal the affirmative advocate has introduced."

The negative advocate then assumes *a* burden of proof on the counter-proposition, but, importantly enough, the affirmative still retains *the* burden of proof on the main or original proposition. If the negative successfully proves the superiority of its counter-proposition over the original proposition, then the affirmative should lose the controversy. The negative advocate must then both show the benefits of his own proposal and stress the liabilities of the original proposal.

The principles can best be understood through examples. A classic example of the counter-proposition can be observed in the strategy of fictional attorney Perry Mason. Mason's client is on trial for murder; prosecution attorney Hamilton Burger presents his usual almost brilliant case proving a murder, a weapon, a motive, premeditation—all of the contentions necessary to the establishment of a *prima-facie* case against Perry Mason's client. Mason has admitted much of Burger's case: a murder, a motive, a weapon. All seems hopeless until Perry uncovers the real murderer, who, as it turns out, wasn't his client at all. In short, Mason introduces a counter-proposition. Not X but Y is the murderer. He then proves the counter-proposition, humiliating Burger once more.

In the case of embezzlement previously mentioned, the defense attorney might conceivably admit to all of the prosecution's case but insist that his client was insane at the time property was misappropriated. Debate on the main proposition would then be suspended while the counter-proposition was argued.

6 / A Study of the Proposition to Determine Its Issues

Only when the advocate has established meaning for his proposition, immersed himself in knowledge relating to the proposition, placed the proposition in its context, and determined the responsibilities of the affirmative and negative advocates should he begin to make definitive judgment as to the issues of the proposition. The discovery and formulation of issues are properly and profitably engaged in only within the climate of prior knowledge and thought.

An issue is a critical question of controversy inherent within the statement of any proposition. What is meant, more precisely, by this definition? The term "critical" suggests the following: (1) A proposition cannot be resolved until its issues are discovered, formulated, studied, and advocated; (2) each issue is *logically* equally important.

Theoretically, the advocate upholding the proposition must establish the validity of his proposition on each issue if he expects to demonstrate the soundness of the proposition.

The term "question of controversy" may be subject to misunderstanding. Although the proposition is phrased in a subjective and didactic way, i.e., it declares a belief is true or an action must be taken, issues are, to the contrary, phrased objectively, inquiringly, impartially. An issue asks a question, a critical question, about the proposition; the advocate who defends the proposition, as well as the advocate denying the proposition, must take a position on the issue, i.e., answer it in terms of his beliefs and commitments. He must then prove the soundness of his position is superior to the soundness of other positions. Hence the issues in a proposition are the same for the advocate defending as well as the advocate attacking the wisdom of the proposition, but the positions taken on the issues will be different because of the controversial nature of critical questions.

The question then arises, since any proposition, as we have seen, arouses dozens of questions, how does one know which of the questions are issues? In short, how does one differentiate a "critical question" from an important question? In a sense the answer is subjective, for it calls into play the matter of personal judgment. There are, however, two guidelines to follow: Critical questions are those which ask something about the proposition itself. Critical questions seek answers necessary to the judicious resolution of the proposition; in short, the outcome of the proposition depends upon the response to the questions. Perhaps an example would help to clarify this point.

If one is arguing for the proposition that the United States should offer birth control aid and advice to requesting nations, he might formulate the following questions in his analysis: Do national economies suffer because of greatly increasing population? Is current food production capable of meeting the demands of today's population, much less the demands ten years hence? Do conditions exist in the world today which make it imperative to control the population explosion? Would a program of disseminating birth control aid and advice be successful? Does high birth rate reduce savings and per capita income in underdeveloped countries? Does population growth increase the threat of war? Would the Peace Corps be an effective instrument for distribution? Would religious groups oppose the proposal? Would the cost of a program to offer aid and advice be prohibitive? Would such a program meet the ethical, moral, and religious values of the people of the United States?

Which, if any, of the above questions are issues? Certainly they all seem important; certainly they all concern some problem associated with the main proposition. But which are critical? Which ask something about the proposition itself? Which will produce answers necessary to the judicious resolution of the proposition? Which could not be answered without committing oneself to an answer on the main proposition?

Using these criteria, the advocate discovers only three issues among the questions: Do conditions exist in the world today which make it imperative to control the population explosion? Would a program of disseminating birth control aid and advice be successful? Would such a program meet the ethical, moral, and religious values of the people of the United States? These three questions ask something of the proposition itself: Is there a pressing need to adopt it? Would it be effective if adopted? Would the program be morally acceptable? The answers to these questions would commit one to a position on the main proposition. A wise decision on the proposition could not be arrived at *until* these questions were answered.

This is not to suggest that the other questions are unimportant. They are important in that they ask questions of the issues, not the main proposition. The answers to them may well lead to the determination of the validity of any position taken on the issues. For instance, an examination of the ability of food production to meet future population needs would be significant in answering the question whether conditions exist which make it imperative to control population growth. But answering this question would not necessarily commit oneself to a position on the main proposition. The same is true regarding the effect of a high birth rate on savings and income in depressed nations. One might agree that a high birth rate reduces savings but at the same time deny that offering birth control aid would be a good policy.

The questions could be structured accordingly:

Should the U. S. offer birth control aid and advice? (proposition)

A. Do conditions exist in the world today which make it imperative to control the population explosion? (issue)

   1. Do national economies suffer because of increasing population? (question about the issue or point in controversy)

   2. Does high birth rate reduce income and savings? (question about the issue)

   3. Does population growth increase the threat of war? (question about the issue)

   4. Is current food production capable of meeting the demands of increasing population? (question about the issue)

B. Would a program of disseminating birth control aid and advice be successful, i.e., would it solve the problems of population explosion? (issue)

   1. Would the Peace Corps be an effective instrument for distribution? (question about the issue)

   2. Would the cost of a program be prohibitive? (question about the issue)

C. Would such a program meet the ethical, moral, and religious values of the people of the United States? (issue)

   1. Could a program not in harmony with accepted values be instituted? (question about the issue)

2. Could such a program be effective? (question about the issue)

One final term in the definition of issue needs brief explanation, and that term is "inherent within the statement of any proposition." One does not manufacture or invent issues, one discovers them. That is to say, they are implicit in the statement of the proposition; one need only locate them.

But how does the advocate discover issues? One approach has already been discussed. Issues are found by asking questions, an outgrowth of analytic research and thought. The questions are then related to each other and the proposition until some sort of hierarchy is established.

A complementary method is that of analyzing the proposition in terms of its classification. In the previous chapter on propositions it was said that the main purpose in classifying propositions was to enable the advocate to discover the issues of a given proposition. There are, you recall, two types of propositions, those of belief and those of action.

The ability to analyze propositions of belief for their issues is extremely important to advocacy, because, first of all, these propositions are encountered more frequently in day-to-day living than any other type of proposition. They exist in and among themselves, but they are also inevitably found as issues in propositions calling for action. One does not face any proposition isolated from his own value system, and, indeed, it is probable that the final decision on any proposition depends more on priorities or beliefs and values than any other single factor. For example, approval or rejection of an international policy of distributing birth control aid may well depend on the resolution of an issue of belief: Is birth control by artificial means morally and ethically acceptable? One could hardly resolve any great proposition without deliberating matters of belief pertaining to it, questions of both fact and value. One works with a belief proposition up to a point in basically the same manner this methodology has suggested so far: He appraises its meaning; he prepares a question memorandum regarding it; he acquires knowledge about it; he attempts to place it in its milieu. From these steps critical questions should begin to emerge.

Issues can be found in propositions of belief through discovering criteria of definition. The attorney who seeks to prove a defendant guilty of embezzlement establishes his issues primarily through *defining* the terms of the charge (or proposition) and applying that definition to the defendant's actions. Embezzlement is (1) the misappropriation of property, (2) by a particular person or persons, (3) without the consent of the owners, (4) for the personal use of the misappropriator. Accordingly, the attorney would raise four issues. (1) Did Mr. X misappropriate designated property? (2) Did he do so without the consent of the owner? (3) Did he take the property for personal use? (4) Did he do so knowingly and willfully? To each issue the prosecuting attorney will answer "yes" and then attempt the proof of his answer. To each issue the defense will answer "no" (in all probability) and then attempt the proof of its position.

In embezzlement the advocate has an immediate external definition (found in the statute) within which he must work. In other cases he must develop his own. The teacher defending the following proposition has a more difficult job: John is guilty of cheating on the final examination in American history. The proposition involves belief through fact and opinion. Having identified John and placed him within the context of the final examination in history, the teacher must then define cheating. Cheating may consist of copying from someone's paper, using material not permitted, talking to another during the examination, having access to the examination before class. The teacher, through defining what it is that John allegedly engaged in, discovers the issues, which might be phrased: Did John copy from someone else's paper during the American history examination? Did John do so deliberately? Did this action constitute a breach of ethics? Note that this proposition of belief is probably an issue leading to a proposition of action: John should be punished.

Let us consider another proposition in which the issues rest on criteria of definition. Suppose you were debating the proposition: Communism constitutes a threat to the internal security of the United States. This is clearly a proposition of belief. One would be concerned, of course, with every term in the proposition, but there is one term which is highly subjective and judgmental, a value-laden term: "constitutes a threat." The word "threat" is of extreme importance. What is meant by "threat"? Rather than arbitrarily defining the word, one might set up criteria, tests by which an item is tried in forming a correct judgment respecting it, to explain what is meant in this particular case by the use of the word. A threat may be said to be that which: (1) has the potential to injure significantly; (2) premeditates to injure; (3) acts to injure significantly. With the criteria thus established, the advocate moves on to the fulfillment of the criteria, and that step involves the second major term in the proposition: "communism," that which is supposedly threatening. To discover whether or not there is a relationship between the subject, communism, and the action, threat, the advocate examines the announced goals of communism, which are (1) overthrow of the government by force, (2) infiltration of political-social institutions. He then proceeds to determine whether or not communism, with these threatening goals, has the potential to achieve the goals and is in the process of attempting to achieve them.

It is entirely possible that in propositions of belief, as well as some propositions of action, there can be more than one set of issues. Each set of issues would satisfy the conditions of being vital questions, equally logically important, and so on, only each would establish the proposition in different ways, depending partially, at least, upon the exact meaning assigned to the proposition by the advocate or analyst. The word "guarantee" in a proposition calling for the Federal government to guarantee a college education to all qualified high school students might imply a guarantee in terms of either civil rights or economic rights, for instance.

In any proposition of action the ultimate issue is one of simple benefit: Would the action be better than present conditions? This answer could be in terms of values, economics, politics, military action, and so forth, and issues might grow out of any one of the value systems employed in the proposition. In propositions of belief, such as a proposition indicating the desirability of disseminating birth control information, issues could be construed for many viewpoints: the problems of world population, the wisdom of family planning in general, whether children should be allowed to come into an evil world, a method which increases man's control over his environment. All issues growing from these viewpoints could be reduced to the concept of benefit. The significant point for the advocate to remember is that through discovering issues, benefit can be established.

How are the issues discovered in propositions of action? Traditionally, a set of issues known as "stock issues" has been automatically applied to any and all propositions of action. Such stock issues are said to be all-inclusive, that is, they constitute a very large tent under which all questions pertinent to a proposition of action can be weighed and discussed. The general wording of these issues is similar to the following:

A. Is the present system unsatisfactory?
   Do evils exist?
   Are the evils serious?
   Are the evils inherent to the system?

B. Is the proposed system an improvement?
    Will the proposal remove the evils?
    Will it result in new and more serious evils?

The approach would appear to be a sound one so long as it is understood fully and so long as it is allowed a certain flexibility. It should not, however, serve to short-circuit the analytic process. One great danger, it would seem, in the use of a formula is that the formula becomes an end in itself rather than a means and that the formula may be instituted in the belief that its use automatically cancels time-consuming processes of thought, research, and plain hard work. The advocate who starts with stock issues rather than arriving at them by an evolutionary process will find himself ill-prepared to advocate the proposition. The use of stock issues, in short, is helpful in that such issues may serve as an *ex-post-facto* check on the advocate's own analytic process, suggesting to him whether or not he is on the "right track" and whether he has included all questions pertinent to the proposition.

The use of preworded questions to be applied to any proposition as issues, in short, still demands an understanding of the nature of the obligation the advocate undertakes in arguing a proposition of action.

In propositions of action the advocate who upholds the proposition is calling for a change in behavior toward a specific policy, a specific way of meeting a problem. He calls for a new approach, a new program, policy, plan, or proposal to meet needs not being adequately met under the *status quo*. Before he can displace presumption and achieve acceptance of his proposal, he must discharge certain obligations. He must present the problem which culminated with the proposition; he must demonstrate that the problems associated with the *status quo* are indeed serious, so serious in fact that the consequences cannot be tolerated, or should not be. He should in many cases show that the consequences affect large numbers of people, i.e., the problem is widespread, hence is a public matter. He should be able to relate the consequences of the problem to valid causes, to identify those causes clearly, and to associate them as an integral part of the *status quo*. He should demonstrate that the problem is so related to current basic theories and ideologies that its solution can come only through broad conceptual changes in both ideology and theory. He must then present a proposal which, through attacking the causes of the problem, will thereby eliminate the unwanted present consequences, producing results that are wanted. Finally, he must show that in the process of eliminating causes and establishing a new approach, his plan will not institute something worse than what is currently unacceptable.

The advocate who understands and accepts these responsibilities and who follows an orderly and knowledgeable system of analysis may, with some degree of safety, at a certain later time in his analytic process, attempt the application of stock issues to a proposition of action, knowing that the stock issue format is supposed to represent a complete system.

A generalized method, however, does not abstract the actual issues of a particular controversy. Therefore, in the process of application the format of stock issues must be adapted to the particular proposition at hand. Hence, in the proposition concerning birth control information, the issues might be stated accordingly:

1. Do conditions exist in the world today which make immediately necessary the dissemination of birth control information and aid on a wide-scale basis?
2. Would the dissemination be in agreement with the ethical, moral, and religious values held by the American people?
3. Would the dissemination of aid and information through the Peace Corps constitute the best plan for meeting the problem on a world-wide scale and, hence, solve the problem?

If an advocate were defending a proposition giving to the state legislature all power to propose and ratify constitutional amendments, the following might be his adaptation to the stock-issue formula:

1. Does the present method of proposing and ratifying constitutional amendments seriously impair the doctrine of states rights and give too much power to the Federal government?
2. Would a proposal whereby state legislatures would have this power and responsibility solve the current problems of the loss of state sovereignty and the growth of federalism without bringing about additional serious problems?

7 / Problems of Continuing Analysis and Counter-analysis

John Stuart Mill wrote of what he termed "continuing criticism and counter-criticism." It was his feeling that the problems of analysis were never resolved until the problem was resolved. That is our feeling, too. As the advocate penetrates the mysteries of his proposition further and further, he should not only expect to revise his earlier analysis of the proposition, but he should demand this act of himself. How frequently does the writer, the scholar, the attorney, the scientist discover upon additional investigation and self-consultation that an earlier held point of view toward a problem or proposition was totally, or in part, erroneous. Sometimes the entirety of the analytic process must be repeated to detect earlier errors; sometimes the remedy is somewhat simpler. Whatever the amount of effort involved, reanalysis in terms of additional research and thought, attacks on previously held positions, and the demonstrated soundness of previously held conclusions, is a necessity.

Depending on the nature of the type of advocacy engaged in, the advocate may or may not come face to face with his adversary, an opposing advocate. But whether or not this happens, the advocate must think and analyze constantly in terms of what an opposing advocate, one taking a position the opposite to that taken by the advocate, has said or written about the proposition, or might say or write about it. The advocate, in short, must put himself in the role of his adversary, and in this role he must ask himself, "If I were arguing against my point of view, against this proposition, what arguments would I use and how would I use them?" Such a listing and appraisal of counter-arguments should lead to additional analysis of one's own position and certainly should lead to a better ability to both defend one's case more effectively and attack the position of the opponent when and if such an attack is called for.

▶ N O T E S ◀

1. John Dewey, *Quest for Certainty* (New York: G. P. Putnam's Sons, 1929), p. 223.
2. Rudolf Carnap, *Philosophy and Logical Syntax* (1935) as quoted in Morton White, *The Age of Analysis* (New York: George Braziller, Inc., 1957), pp. 209-210.
3. Norman K. Smith, *Descartes: Philosophical Writings* (New York: Modern Library, 1958), p. 21.
4. Dewey, *op. cit.*, p. 224.
5. Ludwig Wittgenstein, *Philosophical Investigations* (New York: The Macmillan Company, 1953).
6. Smith, *op. cit.*, p. 14.
7. Bertrand Russell, *A History of Western Philosophy* (New York: Simon and Schuster, Inc., 1945), p. 123.
8. Henry D. Aiken, *The Age of Ideology* (New York: George Braziller, Inc., 1957), p. 73.
9. Nancy Gayer, "Will Existentialism Triumph Over Pragmatism?" *Phi Delta Kappan* (October, 1961), p. 23.
10. *Ibid.*

► EXERCISES ◄

1. What is incorrect in the phrasing of the following propositions relative to the requirements for presumption and burden of proof?

   a. The United States should refuse to recognize Communist China.

   b. The incumbent senator should be returned to Washington.

   c. The United States should discontinue direct economic aid and withdraw all armed forces from Germany.

   d. John Jones is innocent of income tax fraud.

   e. The United States should abolish the "welfare state."

2. The following sets of speeches represent spoken advocacy on significant propositions in American society:

   a. Bernard Baruch, "Atomic Energy Control," *Vital Speeches* (June 14, 1946), Vol. XII, no. 18, pp. 546-551.
   Andrei Gromyko, "Control of Atom Bomb," *Vital Speeches* (June 19, 1946), Vol. XII, no. 18, pp. 551-553.

   b. Winston Churchill, "Alliance of English Speaking People," *Vital Speeches* (March 5, 1946), Vol. XII, no. 11, pp. 329-332.
   Henry A. Wallace, "The Way to Peace," *Vital Speeches* (September 12, 1946), Vol. XII, no. 24, pp. 738-741.

   c. Dean Acheson, "The Atlantic Pact," *Vital Speeches* (March 18, 1949), Vol. XV, no. 12, pp. 355-358.
   Robert A. Taft, "Against the North Atlantic Treaty," *Vital Speeches* (July 11, 1949), Vol. XV, no. 20, pp. 610-617.

   d. Harry S. Truman, "Far Eastern Policy," *Vital Speeches* (April 11, 1951), Vol. XVII, no. 14, pp. 418-420, 422-424.

Robert A. Taft, "The MacArthur Dismissal," *Vital Speeches* (April 12, 1951), Vol. XVII, no. 14, pp. 420-422.

Omar Bradley, "Our World-wide Strategy," *Vital Speeches* (April 17, 1951), Vol. XVII, no. 14, pp. 424-426.

Douglas MacArthur, "Don't Scuttle the Pacific," *Vital Speeches* (April 19, 1951), Vol. XVII, no. 14, pp. 430-433.

e. John F. Kennedy and Richard M. Nixon, "The Presidential Debates of 1960," in Sidney Kraus (ed.), *The Great Debates* (Bloomington, Ind.: Indiana University Press, 1962); *The Joint Appearances of Senator John F. Kennedy and Vice President Richard M. Nixon* (Washington, D.C.: Government Printing Office, 1961).

f. Millard Caldwell, "Judicial Usurpation: The Supreme Court," *Vital Speeches* (January 31, 1964), Vol. XXX, no. 10, pp. 317-320.

Leroy Collins, "The Rights of the States," *Vital Speeches* (December 8, 1963), Vol. XXX, no. 12, pp. 369-372.

g. James William Fulbright, "Foreign Policy: Old Myths and New Realities," *Vital Speeches* (March 25, 1964), Vol. XXX, no. 13, pp. 388-394.

Nelson A. Rockefeller, "Our Foreign Policy: What is it?" *Vital Speeches* (March 3, 1964), Vol. XXX, no. 13, pp. 402-406.

With each set of speeches do the following:

a. Decide the approximate wording of the proposition being argued.
b. Decide if the proposition is one of belief or action.
c. Determine which advocate has the presumption and which has the burden of proof.
d. Discover the full meaning of the proposition (whether or not the advocates realize it) in terms of the language and phrasing.
e. Determine the issues and points-in-support raised by each advocate.

f. Relate the proposition and its analysis to the times in which the advocacy took place. Show what impact the times had on the analysis.

3. Assume that you are an attorney. Into your office comes a man who claims that an editorial in a local newspaper contained certain maliciously false statements about himself. ("Jones is a crook. We've suspected it for a long time, but now we're sure. He should be thrown out of office and asked to leave the community.") As a result of this publication, Jones believes he has suffered great humiliation and damage to his good name, public reputation, and character. He therefore wants to bring suit against the newspaper for compensatory damages and asks you to represent him in court. You accept the case and agree to uphold the proposition: "Fred Jones has been maliciously defamed and subsequently injured by the *Daily News.*" Your responsibility is to prepare and present the best possible case in behalf of this proposition. In relation to the suggested format for analysis in Chapter three, and in terms of the requirements demanded by this specific case, trace the steps you would attempt to follow in the analysis of this proposition of belief.

4. As a class project, select a proposition of belief for research and investigation. The proposition should originate from a current, significant problem. Begin research by tracing the origin of the proposition (as described in Chapter two). Then subject the proposition to close analysis according to the steps in Chapter three.

5. Follow Exercise 4, but use a proposition of action. Of course, a proposition may be selected in which a proposition of belief leads to a proposition of action. Both propositions may be pursued through exercises in following chapters.

► 4 ◄ PROOF THROUGH EVIDENCE

On December 28, 1917, in the midst of World War I, the *New York Evening Mail* published an article by H. L. Mencken purporting to give the "history of the bathtub." The article, later described by Mencken as a "tissue of somewhat heavy absurdities, all of them deliberate and most of them obvious," made such outrageous observations as: the bathtub was unknown until the 1840's; it was invented in Cincinnati by a man named Longsworth; President Fillmore was the first president to take a bath; the bathtub was initially regarded by medical doctors as dangerous to health, and three states had passed laws against its use. Mencken supported his assertions through evidence, which he clearly forged.

According to Mencken 90 per cent of the readers took the article seriously, thereby initiating a seemingly improbable chain of events. He received thousands of letters, most of them either correcting or corroborating his assertions. Chiropractors used his evidence to show the "stupidity of medical doctors"; the article was cited by medical doctors to demonstrate the "progress of public hygiene."

The publication of the article in learned journals soon occurred; it was referred to on the floor of Congress and even finally got into standard works of reference. Mencken himself formally admitted the entire story was a hoax, even writing another article on the repercussions of the first, pointing out the obvious and multitudinous absurdities. But for years after this admission, the conclusions of the article continually appeared in publications as facts of history. As late as 1927 *Scribner's Magazine* published the article in its entirety as authentic, a fact which prompted Mencken to observe, "What remains in the world in the field of wisdom is a series of long-tested and solidly agreeable lies. It is out of such lies that most of the so-called knowledge of humanity flows." People have an instinctive aversion to factual proof, Mencken concluded, but an instinctive frenzy for fictional proof.[1]

THE PROBLEM OF PROOF

A study of argument in history might tend to confirm Mencken's beliefs. Not only has mankind consistently supported his conclusions through fictional and erroneous proof, but he has just as consistently accepted the conclusions of others in much the same way. An assertion in Parson Weems' anecdotal *Life of George Washington* to the effect that young Washington "could not tell a lie" after he cut down the cherry tree became an accepted and credible part of American history, in spite of the fact that Weems' authority for the story was an "aged lady who, as a distant relative, had sometimes visited the Washingtons." The assertion is perhaps innocent, but one could recall many forgeries which could have had, or did have, unfortunate effects. And quite often the inaccuracy and incompleteness of proof is tragic.

On the morning of September 18, 1961, most American newspapers carried the story of the meeting at Ndola, Katanga, between United Nations Secretary General Dag

Hammarskjold and Katangan President Moise Tshombe. The stories did not specify what went on at that meeting, but they were quite similar: the landing of Hammarskjold's plane, the meeting at the airport, the departure of the two men in cars. A few hours later, the evening papers carried an entirely different story, the crash of Mr. Hammarskjold's plane and his untimely death in the jungle. The truth of the matter was that Hammarskjold had never arrived at Ndola, and the proof that he had arrived was false. When the true story was finally told, the reasons for the specious report became clear. Reporters had waited hours for Hammarskjold's arrival; an unmarked plane did arrive, and they assumed it to be Hammarskjold's plane. They saw a party leave the plane to be welcomed; they saw cars drive away. One or more reporters thought they saw Mr. Hammarskjold. Putting their heads together, the reporters came up with one "consistent" story which was dispatched to the world press. The Secretary General's tragic death in the jungle exposed each of the stories as false. While some of the facts were accurate, the inferences and some of the supplied facts were false.

Throughout history the acceptance of assertions and conclusions without evidence at all, or without credible evidence, has resulted in decisions and actions which have led to indescribable human suffering and misery—to wars and material destruction, to political inequalities and the suppression of human rights, to economic catastrophes, to unjust persecutions, to mob violence, and to superstition and prejudice. There is no greater obstacle to the intellectual progress of mankind than man's unwillingness and inability to seek verification of conclusions through evidence.

Each of the above examples contained conclusions which an audience had the right to accept or reject. The conclusions plus evidence and reasoning constituted arguments, and the validity or acceptability of each argument was contingent upon whatever proof the advocate offered in support of his conclusions. To establish his conclusions concerning the history of the bathtub, Mencken manufactured or forged proof. Parson Weems *proved* the cherry tree episode through the authority of an "aged lady." Reporters concluding that Hammarskjold had arrived in Ndola *proved* those conclusions through a chain of misperceptions and circumstantial evidence. In each of the cases the proof offered was inaccurate and incredible, but alarmingly enough, in each case the conclusions were believed, the proof offered seemingly sufficient to gain acceptance for the conclusions.

The thesis of this and the following chapter on proof is that the matter of proof is of such significance to the advocate that he must know its nature and function, as well as its requirements for verification, inordinately well if he is to discharge properly responsibilities to himself, his proposition, and the audience he addresses his conclusions to. The advocate seeks to establish as probably true his proposition and its associated conclusions. As such, he faces sobering responsibilities. Without the use of credible proof his conclusions are merely unsupported assertions or guesses. Without the effective application of proof to any conclusion, the advocate himself cannot know the reliability of that conclusion. He has no inherent right to ask his audience to accept what he himself does not believe to be true. To do so puts the advocate in the role of the demagogue whose desire is to gain believers, not to seek wise decisions.

At the same time, the problem of proof should be of great importance to the audience addressed by the advocate. Many have suggested that the American audience has become so accustomed to hidden persuasion, so victimized by the engineers of consent that it will accept the truth of assertions with virtually no proof except the authority of the advocate, whether he be a news commentator, politician or public figure, or merely a commercial announcer. In short, the American audience has become the constant tool of the propagandist because it has immunized itself from the problems of proof altogether. The evaluation of proof requires analysis and thinking, both seemingly difficult tasks. It is much easier for an audience not to ask how an advocate proved his conclusion. Senator Joe McCarthy proved this point in the early 1950's. Using such devices as a stuffed briefcase, lists of alleged communists, the cropped photograph, and secret documents, McCarthy established an aura of evidence which came to be accepted by many as absolute proof. Professor Barnett Baskerville, of the University of Washington, has termed such devices the "illusion of proof," an illusion designed by an advocate "to produce the shadow but not the substance" in order to mislead people. The illusion of proof is merely a pretense of presenting proof to people who consider themselves rational.[2]

In accepting "proof" based on the authority of the advocate, in accepting illusory proof, the audience debilitates the sanctity of the rational processes, inviting whatever unfortunate consequences that follow. In using his own authority and personality as proof, in substituting illusory proof for rational proof, the advocate refines the art of demagogy and misleads the people.

Proof determines the degree of belief which arises from setting forth the reasons a conclusion should be accepted as probably true. Proof is whatever is necessary to establish the truth claim of an assertion or conclusion.

This chapter is concerned with that aspect of argumentative proof known as evidence.

A RATIONALE FOR EVIDENCE

Argumentatively speaking, the probability or approximation of truth of any given conclusion depends on the validity of the reasoning leading to that conclusion and the adequacy and credibility of the evidence from which the reasoning proceeded.

"Evidence" may be defined as "that form of argumentative proof which deals with facts and opinions as to facts."

All evidence stems from observation of fact; opinion involves one's interpretation of fact, its assimilation, and a resulting conclusion. By "fact" we mean admitted realities. By "opinion" we mean judgment concerning the existence of a fact, a belief about a fact, the interpretation of a fact, or a conclusion about a fact. One must be aware of the role which levels of abstraction play in distinguishing between fact and opinion. As one moves from reporting a fact to framing an opinion about the observed fact, the subjective element becomes stronger; hence accuracy and reliability depend less on quality of observation and more on subjective judgment. Subjectivity becomes far greater, moreover, as one moves into the realm of "synthetic opinion," represented by a prediction or speculation as to future developments. That the population of the world at the present time is approximately 3.16 billion people is a fact, an admitted reality. That an authority would opine that the earth cannot support a population in excess of 3.8 billion people is an opinion, a belief or interpretation about a fact. An opinion is called for when facts are not easily determinable by direct observation. One cannot possibly know for sure what a population in excess of 3.8 billion people would result in, but one can seek the opinion of an expert who, after studying discernable facts, expresses his opinion as to what facts will be at a given time or under given circumstances. Opinion can be directed into the past (e.g., a description of paleolithic culture), or it can be projected into the future. Fact and opinion are relied upon together in the determination of truth.

At a given trial concerning automobile negligence, for example, the ascertainable facts might be that X's car struck Y at an intersection at a given time, that certain physical damages were inflicted upon Y as a consequence, and that X's car suffered certain definable damage. These would be admitted realities. Opinions at the trial would be concerned with the establishment as fact of certain alleged happenings and results—the approximate speed of the car, the attempts of the driver to avoid the accident, the possible negligence on the part of both pedestrian and driver, the emotional damage suffered by Y. Both witnesses and investigating officers would express their opinions as to these alleged facts. The final verdict would reflect the court's opinion as to the truth of the facts presented.

The advocate's main concern in evidence revolves around questions of fact. He seeks facts through either direct observation and reporting or through reliable opinions as to what the facts probably were, are, or will be. Credibility of fact, then, is perhaps the crucial question in evidence. There seems to be sufficient justification for believing that men, although they often err in reasoning, probably possess a capacity which makes them less vulnerable to error in reasoning than in evidence. Man's ability to distinguish fact from fiction, credibility from incredibility, genuineness from forgery, probability from improbability, and reliability from unreliability, as previously discussed, is distressingly vulnerable. The probability of the judgments men make as individuals and as citizens is too frequently restricted by limitations imposed upon the entire reasoning process by the limitations of evidence itself. In propositions of public policy the citizen is confronted with serious problems in locating evidence, interpreting that evidence once it is discovered, using the evidence wisely, and verifying the accuracy of the evidence. These problems, complex and often conflicting, are compounded by the existence of large quantities of information often passed on as evidence. It is little wonder that man errs so often in dealing with evidence.

Yet the advocate cannot abdicate his responsibilities; he must prove his proposition, problems or not, and evidence is indispensable in doing so. He must accordingly learn to locate evidence, to determine its adequacy and credibility, and to learn its proper use in argument.

In our study of evidence we shall consider some presuppositions as to its psychological and semantic variables.

A study of evidential sources and methodologies will follow in which evidence will be appraised as seen by the historian, the attorney, the scientist, and the journalist.

SOME PRESUPPOSITIONS CONCERNING FACT AND OPINION AS TO FACT

To many people there seems little need to dwell on the meaning of fact. A fact is a fact is a fact, they say, and that is all one needs to know. To them anybody can observe a fact; almost anybody can report a fact accurately. The truth of the matter, however, is that a fact is difficult to observe accurately, to perceive correctly, to report honestly, and to verify credibly—all of this in spite of the fact that people use supposed facts as if they were the simplest of all things in the universe.

Psychology has long been interested in problems of fact, particularly in the area of the observation, perception, and reporting of fact. A major psychological concern is in the ability of the individual to differentiate reality from unreality, fact from fiction, and this differentiation involves matters of perception. Perception is said to be the intervening variable between observation of an event and the interpretation of that event. A person may, through his senses —sight, sound, smell, touch—observe an occurrence, but his interpretation of what the event was, what it consisted of, the order of progression, its meaning, and so on will depend upon factors of perception, such as learning, motivation, needs and desires, values—in short, all the personality and social factors through which he must filter the observed event before the event has meaning for him. What is finally perceived is influenced by set, expectancy, and prior experiences, so that, in the words of Gardner Murphy, "perception is more than a passive registration of stimuli impinging on the sense organs. . . ." It consists, Murphy believes, of four stages: ". . . a preparatory stage consisting of expectancy and attending, a sensory reception stage, a trial-and-check stage, and a final structuring stage."[3] The process suggests strongly that what one perceives, or thinks he observes as fact, may often differ wholly or in part from what actually happened, depending entirely on the nature and function of one's filtering system.

Suppose a student demonstration or riot in South Vietnam is observed and reported on by witnesses from the United States (which has invested billions of dollars in that nation in an attempt to keep it out of the Communist bloc), from Communist China (which desires to promote revolution in the country), from a neutral country, say Switzerland, and from South Vietnam itself. The witnesses would have observed essentially the same event, and, assuming them to have observed from a mutual vantage point, they would have had access to the same set of facts. But how different would their perceptions of the riot be? Would each reporter observe and record the same facts? Clearly the facts would to a large degree depend on the perceptions of each reporter, for each reporter would have filtered what he saw and heard through not only his expectancy set, but through prior commitments and beliefs, previous experience and education, as well as a knowledge of the audience to whom he would be communicating his report.

A person's perception of a situation is therefore inextricably linked with his desires, previous experience, and knowledge. One particular variable is often the cause of perceptual distortion and false inferences from perception: the factor of expectancy set. People bring into any situation various readinesses and expectations that govern the manner in which they perceive phenomena. If they are set to respond to a more or less specific stimulus, they may misperceive the wrong stimulus and react to it. A swimmer, set to dive into the water on the sound of a gun, may jump when a door slams. One of the authors of this book stopped at a red traffic light, pushed in the car's cigarette lighter, and waited for the light to change. The lighter popped out and he promptly drove across the intersection! "I was waiting for something to happen," he told his co-author, "and when the lighter jumped out, I started across automatically." These examples illustrate physical set, but mental set may also occur, as when the speaker may give an answer, not to the question asked, but to the question he assumed would be asked.

A person may also be set to expect an event to conform to a theory or attitude. These expectancies may often distort perceptions. Most people have had the experience of eating some food, expecting it to be one dish, and discovering only after several bites that it was something entirely different. The expectancy was so strong that the actual flavor was not at first perceived. In more complex situations when an expectancy set is brought to a situation, the event will tend to be interpreted, usually unconsciously and automatically, to fulfill that expectancy. An ardent Democrat will listen to a speech by a Republican with an expectancy quite different from that of a partisan Republican, and his reporting of the facts of that speech will vary considerably; he will select and interpret them to confirm his expectations. In effect, his expectations tell him what to look for, and so he perceives most clearly those things he is set to perceive.

There are many occasions for inaccurate interpretation resulting from an expectancy set. Everyone is familiar with the stereotyped hypochondriac who reads the medical textbook and "discovers" he or she has the symptoms of a dread disease. (Once a hypochondriac came to a doctor's office and announced that she had Hassenpheffer's disease. "Nonsense," said the doctor. "You wouldn't know if you had it. It has no symptoms." She replied, "My case exactly!") Expectancy is a major process in paranoia. Every event is interpreted to fit and confirm the paranoid's delusions of persecution. If he is criticized, this is direct confirmation; if he is complimented, this proves that people are concealing their intentions. The reporters waiting for Hammerskjold had an expectancy set which distorted their perception and their interpretation of the situation. One of the authors of this book investigated a "haunted house" in which he found that accidents and natural events were misinterpreted to confirm an expectancy that the "supernatural" was present.

Thus, expectancy occurs when one commits himself to a particular theory or hypothesis and then responds to an event in terms of that theory. The event is interpreted and perceived to fit the expectancy or to confirm it, and often this involves actual distortion or misperception of the event. In dealing with evidence, the advocate must continually be aware of the effects of experience, desires, bias, and expectancy on the reporting of events. To assume that anyone can accurately observe, perceive, and describe a given event is an assumption frequently unwisely made.

The relationship between a fact and our response to it has also been the concern of general semanticists, and we will draw on some of their formulations to point out relationships between events and reports which the advocate should keep in mind.[4]

Information is Not the Fact Itself. Implicit in what we have said about evidence is that people report not the fact, but their reaction to the fact. Metaphorically, a report of a fact is like a map of a territory, and just as a map may be inaccurate, distorted, or unrealistic, so may information about a fact. Maps are drawn by persons, and just as a map-maker may draw sea serpents, distort boundary lines, and inadvertently leave out details, so may a reporter invent information, distort happenings, and omit events. The advocate must not equate "what is said" with the event itself, but must recognize that it is a person's reaction to the event.

Reports of Facts are Incomplete. Just as a map cannot include every detail, but is an abstracted or selective picture, so a report cannot include every detail of an observation. No one can possibly know all the facts about anything (despite a recent rash of book titles beginning with "All About . . ."). A person is kept from observing all the facts by his sensory limitations, his physical condition and location, and his environment. He is psychologically limited by his previous experiences, his expectancies, and his biases. He does not remember all he does observe. And few reporters can tell all they know. So the advocate should realize the necessary incompleteness of the information he receives. He must use caution in interpreting it; he must continue to inquire for further facts; and he must not be surprised by additional information.

Our Understanding of Facts Constantly Changes. From the comment that information is necessarily incomplete, it should be obvious that the advocate acts on probabilities, rarely certainties, and his understanding of facts may often change. What was accepted as true yesterday is not sufficiently accurate today. Not only may observations bring new information to change the maps of the territory, but the territory itself may change. A nation's policies, once firm as the earth itself, may change with new leaders. Criminals may become respectable accountants. The soundest industry may be destroyed by technological change. Each fact must be continually reassessed by the advocate. His information must be based on sound observation, complete as possible, as up to date as possible.

THE METHODOLOGY OF EVIDENCE

In a certain sense evidence simply exists; it is up to the researcher, the witness, the advocate, to observe, perceive, record, organize, and use it. There is no discipline, no field of study unconcerned with evidence, for evidence constantly provides proof for the hypotheses of the scientist, the assertions of the historian, the arguments of the attorney, the critiques of the artist and man of letters, the speculations of the journalist, and the conclusions of the social scientist. To the degree that men in each of these areas of learning are concerned with supporting their arguments with evidence and reasoning, each man is the advocate. The student of argumentation rarely concedes that argumentation is his field of study. Rather, he may be a member of the clergy, an historian, an attorney, a scientist, a newspaper reporter, or a citizen engaged in any of society's hundreds of occupations. Nevertheless, in whatever capacity he serves, he becomes from time to time the advocate. As an advocate dealing with the problems of proof, he must turn to his own field of study for both substantive material and methods of interpreting that material, as well as to argumentation for methods of using that material and supporting its use through defending its sufficiency and reliability.

Argumentation as an eclectic discipline draws heavily from other disciplines and areas of study. The student of argument finds that argumentation *per se* is not concerned with amassing a body of material called evidence, but rather with utilization and verification of evidence. In short, argumentation is not a content-oriented discipline, such as history and the sciences, but is more accurately a method-oriented discipline. Saying this does not impugn either the importance or the dignity of argumentation. Evidence is of a very great concern to the advocate, and argumentation teaches him not only its significance, but its use. But argumentation does not provide the advocate with the evidence he must have to support his conclusions.

The advocate then must turn elsewhere for his evidence. He turns to those studies whose essential purpose it is to collect and interpret facts and opinions, and to make that collection available to any student of any discipline for whatever purposes he might need evidence. The advocate employs from time to time evidence from almost every area of study, from the arts, the humanities, and the sciences. He may in his search for proof employ evidence discovered and formulated by the journalist, the scientist, the theologian, the historian, and so on. He goes wherever his need for knowledge takes him, to whatever material is important to the requirements of proof in his proposition.

It seems abundantly clear that the advocate, who utilizes evidence from many different practical sources, must make himself knowledgeable with the rationale the major sources of evidence attach to the gathering of evidence, as well as to its use and validation. If the advocate employs evidence from the behavioral sciences—psychology, anthropology, sociology, politics, etc.—then he surely should have a functional understanding of how the behavioral scientist defines evidence, what his sources for evidence are, in what ways he uses evidence, and how he distinguishes the good evidence from bad. Without this knowledge, the advocate using scientific evidence is like a child playing with a dangerous toy, unaware of its risks.

There are as many approaches to and methodologies of evidence as there are fields of study. It would be an impossible task in a book of this nature to pursue each one. Examination reveals no real need to do so. Most evidence needed and used by the advocate exists in four principal areas of study: history, law, science, and journalism. Additionally, the basic methodologies for finding and verifying evidence are represented by these four areas. To be sure, the reader will discover repetitions in method, but he should also discover broad disagreements in approach. In the end, he should not only be able to properly and thoroughly evaluate the great majority of evidence he runs across in his research, but he should also have made responsible beginnings toward a general methodology of his own. In each of the four areas of evidence the answers to several questions will be sought, although not necessarily *ad seriatim:* What is evidence? What is the function of evidence? What are the sources of evidence? What are the forms of evidence? How does one verify the credibility of evidence?

HISTORICAL EVIDENCE

Facts, facts, whether in the shape of incidents, or opinion, are what I must rely upon: by which I must stand or fall.

William H. Prescott

Historiography is concerned in large part with the discovery, use, and verification of evidence. The historian traces influences, assigns motives, evaluates roles, allocates responsibilities, and juxtaposes events in an attempt to reconstruct the past. That reconstruction is no wiser, no more accurate or dependable than the dependability of the evidence the historian uses for his reconstruction. It is fair to state that questions of evidence are essential to the work of the historian. Arthur Schlesinger, Jr., spoke of the problem this way:

(The historian's task is) . . . to reconstruct the past, to present as truthful a picture as he can of events that have already taken place. In performing this task, the historian requires, above all, evidence. It is the character of the evidence which establishes the framework within which he writes. He cannot imagine scenes for which he has no citation, invent dialogue for which he has no text, assume relationships for which he has no warrant. Fact is his raw material, and the farther he strays from his evidence, the more contentious his history becomes.[5]

How successful is the historian in recreating objective reality? Schlesinger, among many others, feels the quest for evidence is not always rewarding: "The sad fact is that, in many cases, the basic evidence for the historian's reconstruction of the really hard cases does not exist, and the evidence that does exist is often incomplete, misleading, or erroneous."[6] Historian Louis Gottschalk, however, denies that the historian seeks objective reality in his evidence. "The facts of history . . . are the facts of meaning," he writes, and the historian attempts to reconstruct only as much of the past as can be accurately reconstructed.[7] But whether the historian seeks objective reality or the facts of meaning, he must first begin with sources.

The extensiveness of these sources is already staggering, and the amount of accumulated material grows steadily. Alan Nevins estimates that there are from thirteen to fourteen thousand books published per year which might be of interest and use to the historian, as well as literally hundreds of thousands of articles, monographs, and other historical works and documents.

In spite of this massive accumulation of evidence, Nevins tends to agree with Schlesinger as to its insufficiency:

The difficulty which most frequently daunts the historian in dealing with evidence, is precisely that which most often disturbs judge and jury: there is not enough of it. Rarely indeed do we encounter a historical event of importance regarding which *all* the pertinent facts are known; all too frequently we are nonplused by transactions whose most vital particulars are missing. History is frequently an attempt to find correct answers to equations which have been half erased. And in addition to the paucity of evidence, historical students must often lament its bad quality. Even when it exists with a fair degree of technical integrity, it is not unlikely to be evidence of a type which a keen opposing attorney could riddle with holes.[8]

First of all, then, the advocate should recognize what the historian readily admits: evidence is frequently insufficient to warrant conclusions. Evidence is frequently of such poor quality that its lack of credibility precludes its honest use. Evidence is often quite inconclusive, i.e., from it there is difficulty in drawing any conclusion.

The problems of determining both sufficiency and credibility are problems of "verification" to the historian. In some way he must examine historical evidence for its authenticity, its dependability, and its adequacy. In the process of examination the historian exercises both *external* and *internal* tests of criteria. External criticism of evidence involves questions relating to the source of evidence, while internal criticism deals with the nature of the evidence itself, an analysis of the document for credibility. In employing both these tests the historian has a basic point of view: "Be skeptical. Regard every assertion with doubt." In short, every piece of evidence should be considered guilty until proven otherwise. The rule is one worth remembering for the advocate.

Gottschalk and Nevins both suggest a methodology for external criticism. In attempting to establish the credibility of evidence through the reliability of its source, the advocate should ask the following questions: What are the credentials of the reporter of the evidence? How did the reporter arrive at the evidence? Was he willing and able to tell the truth? Is there independent corroboration for the evidence?

The Credentials of the Reporter. The first task is that of establishing the identity of the author of the evidence, and the date of his testimony. Not all men are qualified to give competent and reliable testimony. The historian asks about the witness: Is the witness possessed of the knowledge and experience necessary to qualify him as reliable? Is the witness a schooled or experienced observer and reporter? The hypothesis is that the evidence of a schooled, experienced reporter is generally superior to that of the untrained and casual observer. The greater the expertness of the reporter in the matter which he reports, the more reliable the report. (A veteran policeman observing an accident would probably write a more reliable report on the accident than a bystander observing the same accident.) The historian also takes into account the general character and reputation of the witness, as well as his purpose in writing or speaking about an event. The greater the reporter's reputation for honesty and accuracy, the greater the reliability of his report.

Important to the assessment of the character of the witness is the question pertaining to why he reported the event and for whom he intended his report. Some records are intended for propaganda purposes or to answer objections and arguments raised by others. The general rule is that the more serious the author's intention to make a mere record, the more dependable his evidence as a historical source.[9] A writer who entered an event in his diary intending no one but himself to read the entry, or a reporter who wrote about an incident to a friend, would probably write a more accurate description of the event than a reporter covering the event for a newspaper. Generally speaking, the fewer the number for whose eyes a document was intended (the greater its confidential nature, in other words), the more naked its contents are apt to be.

The Reporter and His Observations. How did the reporter arrive at the evidence? Was he an eyewitness to the events he narrated? If not, what were his sources of information? It almost goes without saying that a direct observer of an event can be depended upon to furnish a more accurate and dependable description of it than the observer who got his information from a second party. How much time elapsed between the reported event, or observation, and the recording of it? The historian assumes that reliability is inversely proportional to the time lapse between an event and the recollection of that event. The closer the report to the event, the higher the degree of credibility.

Willingness and Ability to Tell the Truth. The best evidence, writes Nevins, "is that in which no element of self-interest, no element of ignorance, and no element of bias appears."[10] Credibility, then, would depend to a great degree on whether or not a witness wanted to tell the truth, and, if he wanted to, whether or not he was free to tell the truth.

A witness' ability to tell the truth depends on his possession of whatever senses (sight, sound, smell, touch) that were necessary to enable him to observe an event; his ability to tell the truth would depend likewise on his experience, his state of mental health, his character, and the degree of attention paid to the event by the witness at the time he observed it.

The witness' willingness to tell the truth is perhaps the most challenging question of all: Did he engage consciously or unconsciously in falsehood? Of chief concern in answering the question is an evaluation of the nature of the biases of the witness as applied to that which he reports. Tacitus wrote that he would compose history *sine studio et ira, studium* being a bias favorable to a subject, and *ira* being a bias unfavorable. He thus put himself on record as the "disinterested witness." The historian seeks the disinterested witness, but, at the same time, he realizes such a witness never really exists. Accordingly he asks of each witness: To what degree is he interested? In what ways might he benefit from slanting the truth? Therefore, why might he desire, consciously or unconsciously, to bias his testimony?

The presence of bias in all testimony presents enormous problems in verification. The advocate should understand, as does the historian, that all evidence is colored more or less by the testifier's emotions, his personal involvement, and his group affiliations. The significance of these biases, of course, varies from person to person and from evidence to evidence. But the advocate can be reasonably sure that every person, in his attitudes toward personal and social issues, speaks to a degree from his biases, from a set of predetermined convictions. The advocate's responsibility is to discover these subjective influences and to weigh all evidence carefully in terms of his appraisal of their importance.

In dealing with biases a scientific attitude is called for. The advocate must develop analytical habits of mind, examining the character and personality of the witness, as well as his social, ethical, political, and economic background and his group affiliations (racial, national, class, professional or vocational, etc.). He must become aware of the environment in which the witness wrote and his involvement and predisposition toward the event or issue on which he wrote. He must recognize what Gottschalk has termed the "clearest mark of the biased witness,"[11] that is, his desire to oversimplify events, to look for the single causative factor which explains everything. Thus will people attempt the explanation of both domestic and foreign problems by attributing those problems to one cause, communism. Or those who believe in state supremacy will attribute multiple problems to one cause, the growth of Federal power.

Independent Corroboration. The historian seeks to find external and independent corroboration for his evidence. Gottschalk spells out the general rule of historians, which is "to accept as historical only particulars which rest upon *the independent testimony of two or more witnesses.*"[12] In cases where two witnesses agree, they may agree because they may have put their heads together beforehand, as was the case with the reporters writing of the arrival of Mr. Hammarskjold. Or one may have copied from the other. Until and unless independence as observers is established, as Gottschalk suggests, "agreement may be confirmation of a lie or of a mistake rather than corroboration of a fact."[13]

Sometimes corroboration is impossible and the historian may have to turn to a document's general credibility or the author's reputation for veracity. Such approaches may well be satisfactory. When a direct conflict of testimony exists, that is, one source says one thing and a second source says something just the opposite, the problem of external corroboration becomes acute. The historian must then not only seek the views of an independent source, but he must study the pieces of evidence carefully in terms of their internal nature.

Let us now turn to problems of *internal* criticism. One of the tasks of internal criticism is that of determining whether the evidence is forged or misrepresened. History abounds with forgeries and misrepresentations, either deliberate or unintentional. Several purposed "diaries" of Napoleon confused historians for years. And historians still argue as to the authenticity of the "Casket Letters," letters allegedly written by Mary Queen of Scots to her lover Bothwell. How does the historian go about the determination of forgery? A classic example is the method through which historian Paul Angle exposed as fraudulent the allegedly authentic correspondence between Abraham Lincoln and Ann Rutledge. In 1928 the *Atlantic Monthly* published supposedly authentic letters exchanged between Lincoln and Miss Rutledge. The letters not only deceived the editors of the magazine, but even the Lincoln scholar Carl Sandburg. Historian Angle examined the forgeries carefully, and in an article in *Atlantic Monthly* a year later exposed them. He had examined the paper on which the letters were written and concluded the paper bore the appearance of flyleaves torn from old books. The ink, he reported, contained aniline dye, a dye unknown before 1850. The handwriting of Lincoln did not match other specimens of Lincoln's handwriting. Stylistic differences between the letters and Lincoln's other writings were obvious. The contents of the letters were frequently inconsistent with Lincoln's known views on public issues. Historical inconsistencies were frequent and significant. These and other findings led Professor Angle to deny the authenticity of the correspondence, a fact later agreed to by the writer of the correspondence.[14] The advocate should observe Angle's method.

A second problem of internal criticism relates to meaning. Once the historian assures himself that his evidence is neither forged nor misrepresented, he moves on to determine the meaning of that evidence. He is, of course, primarily concerned with what the evidence says, but he may not be able to abstract meaning without a knowledge of the writer and his style and the period in which the writer wrote. The historian, as the advocate, must determine not only what the words of the testimony formally mean, but what the author intended them to mean. Once meaning is reasonably understood, the historian seeks to examine that meaning for credibility. How does he go about doing this?

He goes about doing it, as Gottschalk explains, by answering the question: Is this particular credible? What Professor Gottschalk means by credible is, "not that it actually happened, but that it is as close to what happened as we can learn from a critical examination. . . ."[15] The concern is with verisimilitude rather than truth, and, although there may be a high correlation between the two, they are not necessarily identical.

The following questions may be put to the evidence in question: (1) Does the evidence appear to be the result of an opportunity to know the truth plus thorough investigation? (2) Is there lack of self-contradiction within the evidence? (3) Is there absence of contradiction in other consulted sources? (4) Does the evidence conform to or agree with other known facts? (5) Is the evidence of a general or specific nature? (6) Are the separate details of the evidence in themselves credible? (The general credibility of a document, it is believed, can be no better than the credibility of the separate details: *falsus in uno; falsus in omnibus!*)

The rules for external and internal criticism of historical evidence, although formulated by historians for the use of historical scholars, are applicable to the advocate when he deals with historical evidence. There are many of the rules which the advocate may readily and successfully apply to a great deal of the evidence he comes into contact with. The close analysis of the evidence itself on an *ad hoc* basis, as well as the careful examination of the witnesses' qualifications and biases, constitute valuable evidential tools for any advocate. Through their use the advocate can make his conclusions, as Nevins phrased it, the "measure of sound grain sifted by rigorous criticism from the straw and chaff of good, bad, and indifferent testimony."[16]

LEGAL EVIDENCE

It is often said that the evidence of law is the evidence of the advocate, that the advocate defending a proposition of public policy approaches evidence in much the same way as the attorney defending his client. The statement appears to be both true and false. To the extent that all advocates seek the support of their conclusions through evidence, there is a similarity between the public advocate and the legal advocate. But, as we shall see in the discussion of legal evidence, in many ways legal evidence is far too absolute, far too rigid for the needs of the ordinary advocate. Nevertheless, there is much the advocate can learn about the use and verification of evidence through a study of law.

Law is concerned with evidence in two vital areas: (1) evidence consisting of precedent growing out of former decisions rendered in courts on various civil and criminal controversies and (2) evidence in the form of proof introduced in a specific case to establish the guilt or innocence (in criminal cases) or the liability or non-liability (in civil matters) of particular defendants. Evidence in the former case constitutes *corpus juris,* the body of the law, the total collection of the law, and from this compilation of evidence precedents are drawn which are applied to specific alleged violations of the law. A case may be decided on the evidence of a finding of a court in a previous similar case; laws are interpreted on the basis of evidence handed down by the Supreme Court in a past decision. Evidence in the latter case constitutes facts and opinions directly related to a present particular case under consideration by the court.

The advocate in supporting many propositions will be concerned with precedent, with the significance of prior court decisions and holdings. The findings of the courts in almost every area of society constitute evidence and support for or against propositions of action and belief. An advocate supporting a program of Federal aid to education would need to know what evidence, in the form of court decisions, was germaine to his arguments, just as the advocate attorney must study previous court decisions on defamation if he is to wisely defend a client accused of defamation. The evidence of legal precedent speaks for itself; it is, in a sense, historical evidence in the form of public records. It appears to require only recognition, not appraisal and evaluation.

Evidence pertaining to a specific trial in court, however, must demand and receive great attention, for it is this evidence which warrants the particular decision on a case which eventually becomes a precedent.

Because of the fact that law deals with issues of human life and property, it has established through the years an evidential system which is rigid and inflexible, a system which imposes severe ultimate tests on the acceptability and probative value of all evidence. Law assumes an evidential approach which presumes that all testimony of all witnesses is suspect if an attorney can impugn their general character or create any doubt as to their veracity. Great concern is afforded both witness and document, and considerable emphasis is placed on corroborative evidence. In all criminal cases evidence must be of such a nature as to establish "substantial certainty" concerning the existence of facts (as opposed to civil cases in which a high degree of probability must be established). In short, evidential law imposes a rigidity seldom encountered in other disciplines.

Blackstone defined "evidence" as "that which makes clear or ascertains the truth of the very fact or point in issue, either on the one side or the other."[17] James Bradley Thayer discussed the nature of legal evidence in a revealing passage:

What is our law of evidence? It is a set of rules which has to do with judicial investigations into questions of fact. . . . These rules relate to the mode of ascertaining an unknown, and generally a disputed matter of fact. . . . When one offers evidence, he offers to prove, otherwise than by mere reasoning from what is already known, a matter of fact to be used as a basis of inference to another matter of fact. . . . In giving evidence we are furnishing to a tribunal a new basis for reasoning.[18]

John Henry Wigmore, who compiled a five-volume study of evidence, adds one additional element to Thayer's definition, an element of some importance to the advocate. Wigmore considered evidence to be any knowable fact or group of facts considered with a view to its being offered to a legal tribunal, "for the purpose of producing a persuasion as to the truth of a proposition on which the determination of the tribunal is to be asked."

Legal evidence, then, seeks to affirm or deny a conclusion through comment on its truth. It consists of sets of rules which are applicable to the admissibility of facts and opinions in court which seek support for an unknown and disputed matter of fact. The purpose of evidence is to produce persuasion as to the truth of a conclusion.

Sets of rules concerning the admissibility, credibility, function, impeachment, and rehabilitation of evidence have evolved over a period of centuries. Legal rules of evidence have multiple concerns, of course, but chief among them are three: What facts may be presented as evidence? By whom must evidence be presented? To whom must evidence be presented? The legal advocate concerned with the proof of a given conclusion must demonstrate: (1) that certain facts or groups of facts exist; (2) that to the contingency of their existence the state attaches the legal consequences asserted by the claimant. Both demonstrations require evidence.

What are the forms of legal evidence? Wigmore classified all legal evidence in the following categories:

1. The presentation of the thing itself as to which persuasion is desired, such as a weapon, broken leg, document, premises on which an act was committed, and scene of an accident. Such evidence is *presumptive* evidence, or *real,* evidence (autoptic).
2. The presentation of some independent fact by inference from which the persuasion is to be produced. This is *inferential* evidence, and consists of two forms:

    a. Direct, or *testimonial,* evidence—the assertion of a human being as to the existence of the thing at issue.

    b. Indirect, or *circumstantial,* evidence—evidence which suggests a fact at issue is true through the establishment of circumstances or facts which afford a basis for a reasonable inference of a connection between facts which are known and those that are unknown.[19]

Presumptive evidence is almost self-explanatory. Through such evidence certain facts are proved *per se* (by their very existence). A contract between plaintiff and defendant would be presumptive evidence; there would seldom be a question of relevancy concerning the production of a contract in a case, and its acceptability would lead to the establishment of facts concerning whether or not the contract has been broken or should be broken. Direct evidence proves or disproves itself (*res ipsa loquitur*), although there may from time to time be questions relating to the authenticity of a document, the ownership of a weapon, the extensiveness of physical injury, and so on. Presumptive evidence is difficult to impeach.

Inferential evidence, on the other hand, is highly subject to impeachment. That evidence which involves reasoning from some fact to the proposition itself is said to be inferential, whether the fact is arrived at through direct testimony of a witness or through circumstantial, or indirect, ways. One must be careful to distinguish testimonial from circumstantial. In his book *Evidence* Thomas Starkie drew this differentiation:

Where knowledge cannot be acquired by means of actual and personal observation, there are but two modes by which the existence of a bygone fact can be ascertained: first, by information derived either immediately or mediately from those who had actual knowledge of the fact (testimonial); or secondly, by means of inferences or conclusions drawn from other facts connected with the principal fact which can be sufficiently established (circumstantial). In the first case, the inference is founded on a principle of faith, in human veracity, sanctioned by experience. In the second, the conclusion is one derived by the aids of experience and reason from the connection between the facts which are known and that which is unknown.[20]

An accused might be convicted of taking funds from a company safe by direct testimony, e.g., a fellow employee testifies that he saw the accused open the safe and take the money. Or an accused might be convicted of taking funds from a company safe through circumstantial evidence, e.g., a witness testifies that the accused told him he had great need of money. Another witness testifies that the accused recently paid him a great deal of money. A third witness testifies that the accused worked late on the night the company safe was robbed. Through inferences drawn from the testimony of these witnesses a jury might decide that the accused was guilty of robbery, even though no one had seen him perform the act.

In both direct and circumstantial evidence the court maintains two concerns, one relating to the admissibility of evidence, the other concerning the value of evidence once it has been admitted. It is important to distinguish, as the attorney must, between the quite separate factors of admissibility and credibility of evidence. Some disabilities will affect both features of a piece of evidence; others will affect only one or the other. The tendency in law is to allow the presentation of evidence but to permit comment on its possible lack of credibility and leave the judgment to the jury. The court wants to listen to any person and hear any evidence pertinent to any item of fact being considered by the court. Some evidence the court will eventually reject, and some will be accepted. But the court wishes to hear all evidence worth listening to, not presuming to know ahead of time what testimony will be correct or what testimony will be incorrect. Accordingly, the court's first concern regarding witness and testimony is the relevancy and admissibility of that testimony from that particular witness. Relevancy, of course, is not the only obstacle to admissibility. Equally as important is whether or not the evidence is "hearsay," i.e., did it come to the witness through another party rather than being directly observed? The court asks: Is the witness qualified sufficiently to be allowed to testify concerning a fact or facts pertaining to a particular case? Was the witness a direct observer of the facts he is to attest to? Answering the questions does not imply that the evidence the witness is to give is good or bad, it signifies merely that the evidence is worthy of being received by the court for the purpose of being weighed along with all the other evidence: It is relevant; it is not hearsay. Wigmore put it this way:

When the court declares testimony admissible, it declares implicitly that the sanity, experience, knowledge, etc., of the witness are such that the hypotheses of the assertion being idle chatter, ignorant gossip, or otherwise untrustworthy, are sufficiently negative *prima facie*, and that the assertion is *prima facie* worth listening to.[21]

The court, in other words, merely inquires whether experience and precedent have sanctioned certain conditions which must accompany the evidence.

The three elementary criteria basic to admissibility are:

(1) The witness must know something, i.e., observed raw data.

(2) The witness must have a recollection of these observations.

(3) The witness must be able and willing to accurately communicate these recollections.

Once admitted, the credibility of the testimony comes under consideration. Two important sets of questions relate to the expertness of the witness and his moral character:

The first set of questions concerns the experiential capacity of the witness, his particular skill to acquire certain accurate conceptions. Involved here are matters of expertness, fitness to answer, special qualifications which tend to make some testimony more valuable than other. In a sense it is misleading to think of some witnesses as "expert" and others as "ordinary." In a strict sense every witness is an expert, i.e., he possesses special knowledge on a subject. But law differentiates, and an expert witness is one whose fitness by reason of the subject matter needs to be first shown. That fitness may come from occupational experience or from systematic training. A lumberman testifying as to the type of lumber in a ladder used for kidnapping purposes would be an expert witness, and his testimony would possess unusual value. A county assessor testifying as to the value of a piece of property would be an expert. The value of expert testimony lies in the difficulty of impeaching it.

A second set of questions to be applied to the credibility of evidence concerns the moral qualifications of the witness. Certain witnesses are alleged not to possess the character and reputation necessary to assure their veracity and reliability on the witness stand. Has the witness been convicted of a previous crime that might suggest his unreliability, e.g., fraud or perjury? Does the witness have special interests in the outcome of the case? Does the witness possess biases which could impugn the veracity of his testimony?

The problems of credibility of evidence in cases where emphasis must of necessity be placed on indirect or circumstantial evidence are deserving of special consideration, for circumstantial evidence possesses problems all its own. Professor Wigmore has indicated three types of circumstantial evidence: prospectant, concomitant, and retrospective. A better understanding of the meaning of these types may come from applying them to a specific case. Judge Alton B. Parker, long-time New York attorney and Democratic candidate for President in 1904, once told of a case he was familiar with that demonstrated the effective use of circumstantial evidence. (The judge strongly believed in the probative value of circumstantial evidence.) The story concerned the judge's first murder case. A defendant was put on trial for killing a woman in upstate New York. Nobody witnessed the killing; there was no direct evidence. In the trial that followed, however, the following facts were brought forth (testimony which, incidentally, circumvented the *hearsay* rule): The defendant bought powder and shot at a local store; he expressed to friends his dislike for the deceased as well as his need for money; he borrowed a shotgun from a resident of the community; for wadding he tore a page from a copy of a magazine subscribed to by the man he borrowed the gun from, using one half of the page for wadding and pocketing the other half; he was seen approaching and leaving the deceased's home on the night of the murder; he tried to spend a five-dollar bill, a counterfeit bill known to belong to the deceased; the wadding was found near the body of the deceased, and the other half found in the defendant's pocket, along with the five-dollar bill he had tried to get rid of. From this circumstantial evidence, the man was convicted and hanged. Judge Parker held such evidence to be conclusive.

Applying the three types of circumstantial evidence to this particular case we find:

(1) *Prospectant*—the design to perform an act, as seen above in the purchase of powder and shot and the borrowing of a gun; in addition to the presence of a motive, as seen in anger expressed for the deceased and the need for money.

(2) *Concomitant*—testimony to the fact that the defendant entered and left the deceased's house on the night of the murder.

(3) *Retrospective*—after-the-event facts, as seen in the wadding found near the body which matched wadding found on the defendant, the defendant's attempt to spend the five-dollar counterfeit bill, and his attempt to get rid of the bill which was subsequently found in his possession.

The advocate should make a similar delineation in dealing with propositions which must be largely proven through circumstantial evidence. Prospectant evidence requires the admissibility of evidence relating to the character and disposition, habits, emotions, motives, designs, and even physical capacity of involved persons. Concomitant evidence demands the reconstruction of facts which are thought of as being in existence at the time of and in connection with the act to be proven: Did the defendant have opportunity to perform the act in question? Could others have had equal opportunity? Do any facts exist which cannot co-exist with the performing of the act in question? (e.g., Does the defendant have an alibi? Did a third party confess to the act in question? Might the act be self-inflicted?) Retrospective evidence looks backward from the evidential fact to the alleged act, inferring from it that at some previous time the act was or was not performed. Items such as consciousness of guilt or innocence, behavior of involved persons after the act in question, and mechanical traces, such as the possession of documents, weapons, equipment, and so forth. All of these items can be employed as a basis of an inference that the person performed the act with which circumstances are associated. The admissibility of such evidence is ordinarily more difficult to achieve because of the problems of establishing relevancy. The advocate must be able to relate the evidence to the proposition in such a way that the evidence is vital to the proof of the proposition.

It is the responsibility of the court (a jury in some cases, a judge in others) to pass final judgment on the credibility of all specific evidence and on the probative nature of the whole body of evidence presented by both sides to a controversy. The processes of a trial so function that this responsibility can be discharged in an orderly manner which permits the careful evaluation of all witnesses and all testimony. Each witness is questioned directly, and all evidence he gives is subjected to cross-examination by an opposing attorney. The attorney calling the witness has as his purpose the eliciting of whatever testimony he thinks is appropriate and necessary to support his contentions. He attempts to corroborate as much testimony as possible through real evidence and additional testimony of other witnesses. He resupports or rehabilitates this evidence to the best of his ability after the evidence has undergone cross-examination. The opposing attorney has the task of impeaching whatever evidence he has reason to doubt the veracity of, whether his doubt comes from the lack of qualifications of the witness or the possible incredible nature of the evidence itself. Thus, through this exacting process, the belief exists that truth will somehow emerge concerning the goodness or badness, reliability or unreliability of the evidence itself.

Differentiating good from bad evidence, in the final analysis, must be the subjectively oriented task of a jury or judge, no matter how rigorously the attorneys have conducted their examinations and cross-examinations. Only those people on whose consciences the final decision rests can eventually decide which evidence was credible and which was not. Verification of legal evidence, then, is in a very real sense a subjective experience. No hard-and-fast rules exist by which the court can distinguish good from bad. But precedent and common sense clearly establish certain presuppositions and criteria which can be of assistance in the determination. A jury would surely be concerned with the organic tests, such as the sanity of a witness, his intelligence, his ability to remember, and his possession of whatever senses are necessary to make him an accurate observer. A jury would likewise concern itself with certain moral tests: the biases of the witness, his involvement in the outcome of the case, his character and previous behavior, his ability and willingness to tell the truth. A jury would take into consideration both the degree of expertness from which a witness spoke and its own appraisal of the knowledge of the witness—his opportunity to observe the fact in question. These matters would directly affect the credibility of testimony.

At the beginning of this study of legal evidence the suggestion was made that perhaps legal evidence was a type too rigid and formal for its complete adoption by the ordinary advocate. To be sure, the advocate is concerned with problems of admissibility of evidence, and although he may require many of the tests the attorney requires, he will not as a rule require them all in the establishment of probability. Moreover, he will be less exacting in the degree to which his evidence conforms to the rules, since he deals not with substantial certainty, but with probability. In short, his ultimate tests will usually be less severe than those of the attorney.

In terms of the rules of verification of the evidence itself for credibility the advocate can afford to be likewise less rigid than the attorney. Moreover, the advocate can often give weight to the inherent evidence of the situation, whereas in law this cannot be done. If, for example, the advocate discovered conflicting and contradictory evidence from two sources, both reliable, he could examine the character, background, and behavior of both witnesses and through such an examination reach conclusions as to which witness was probably telling the truth. The advocate concerned with the conflicting testimony of General Douglas MacArthur and President Harry Truman about what was said at Wake Island in the autumn of 1950 would be free to assess the motives and reputation of each man. In the absence of corroborative testimony the advocate might well reach a probable conclusion on the basis of the evaluation of MacArthur's propensity for telling the truth plus whatever reasons he might have had for not telling the truth about the Wake conference. In law such emphasis on the inherent evidence would not be permissible. If a man were accused of assault (threatening another with violence), he could not be convicted of battery simply on the oath of a single witness in court, nor is it likely that he would be convicted through a study of the inherent evidence. The corroboration of an independent witness would be necessary.

Finally, there is certain evidence valuable to the advocate which would be rejected by a court. Incomplete evidence is often credible and useful to the advocate. Whereas an attorney could not, in the trial of an alleged drunken driver, use testimony to the effect that the driver had previously been convicted of automobile theft (such evidence would not only be incomplete, but inherently and highly prejudicial, more likely to be harmful than probative), the advocate could certainly establish the fact that the witness used by his adversary had consistently been in error in matters of opinion in the past.

Most of the limitations imposed on the use of legal evidence stem from one basic consideration, the fact that the law wishes to deal with absolutes, incontrovertible conclusions, whereas the ordinary advocate, dealing essentially with problems of public policy, seeks the establishment not of absolutes, but of degrees of high probability. Differences in the demands concerning both quantity and quality of evidence are reflected accordingly.

SCIENTIFIC EVIDENCE

Unfortunately, research evidence from the sciences rarely plays an important role in public advocacy, despite the fact that science has in large part created the major conflicts of our times and can at least partially resolve them. The physical, biological, and behavioral scientific disciplines can also shed light on many conditions of which science was not the creator. Advocates who use evidence from science are using one of the single most powerful tools we have for understanding and controlling contemporary reality.

Barriers to disarmament cannot be fully comprehended without knowledge of weapons system performance, seismometrical and radiation monitoring techniques, and the broader problem of reducing psychological tension.[22] Population explosion is a demographical-biological problem as well as a political and moral one. Free speech involves more than ethics and the law; integral to its understanding is knowledge of the processes and effects of mass communications, group conformity, and crowd hysteria. Underdeveloped nations can best be assisted if the factors considered include industrial technology, public health, ecology, social diffusion theory, and anthropological and psychological aspects of education and communication. In the United States a frequently debated proposition is: "Why Johnny can't read," or more generally: "Why Johnny doesn't learn." Educational psychology and sociology are disciplines most able to explain innate and environmental causes behind Johnny's behavioral difficulties. Unfortunately, however, advocates usually ignore the findings of these disciplines, turning instead to the testimony of administrators and miscellaneous amateur "experts," many of whom exhibit a quite transparent political-philosophical prejudice.

Any proposition, along with its issues, is complex, and must therefore deserve an eclectic treatment, as we have previously observed. Eclecticism does not stop, as most advocates seem to think, after one has surveyed history, economics, law, and amateur expertise. The frequent absence of evidence from science in the argumentation of our society is a sign of a basic and seemingly pathological ignorance. Harvard physicist Gerald Holton is one of many who believe society is in danger of losing contact with our environment: "The brutal fact is that, by losing contact with even the elementary facts of modern science, our intellectuals, for the first time, are losing their hold on the world."[23]

The intellectual advocate is the educator of the citizen. If he can no longer see the way, there is little hope that the rest of mankind can do any better. And if society cannot see the way, it may not long stay away from the ever-present abyss which seems to be an integral feature of the twentieth century. British novelist and physicist Charles P.

Snow has spoken wisely of the dangers of the gap between science and citizen:

When those two senses have grown apart, then no society is going to think with wisdom. For the sake of the intellectual life, for the sake of the Western society living precariously rich among the poor, for the sake of the poor who needn't be poor if there is intelligence in the world, it is obligatory for us and the Americans and the whole West to look at our education with fresh eyes. . . . We have very little time. So little time that I dare not guess at it.[24]

The advocate, as educator and influencer, must take the lead by turning more and more to science as a source of evidence. But it is not enough to use scientific evidence; one must be able to use it responsibly. All too often advocates fail to do so. Most do not adequately discriminate between the *scientific image*, or aura, and the *scientific attitude*. The scientific image is a majestic façade of omnipotence and omni-accuracy which becomes indiscriminately attached to scientists, popularizers, and quacks whenever they "sound" scientific. There have been frequent times in the history of this country during which the phrase "science tells us" was sufficient *per se* to prove anything from the origin of man to the orgies of the 1920's. The scientific image proved anything, even if the scientific attitude couldn't. And any and all evidence from science was accepted without question as proof for the establishment of an indefinite number of arguments.

The scientific *attitude* is quite different. In essence it is an outlook of suspended judgment, of waiting until all the available data has been found before drawing conclusions. (One should differentiate between scientific attitude and scientific method. We term the approach an "attitude" because it does not *always* employ a rigid set of procedures, steps, etc., that have become identified with the scientific method, as popularly propagated.) Conclusions arrived at by those using the scientific attitude are never irrevocable, and they are not treated as such. The body of knowledge of a science is always in the process of being subjected and resubjected to logical and empirical checks or tests of validity. A cardinal advantage of the scientific approach is that it has yielded theories which enable men to predict more accurately what will happen in the future than does any other means. But these theories were not arrived at quickly, only by painstaking, step-by-step study. Conclusions were not quickly reached. The power of science to predict has come from science's reluctance to predict.

Often it is not easy to know whether or not the scientific attitude is being employed. More and more frequently the public faces a controversy produced by the scientist who, after gaining a reputation for using the attitude scrupulously in his research work, speaks out on political and moral issues in public in a somewhat less restrained manner. Former chairman of the Atomic Energy Commission David E. Lilienthal recently wrote of this problem. Referring to a "crisis of confidence," which had its roots in concern that scientists have more and more been seeking to use methods applicable to the physical world in areas of the world of men beyond the reach of such methods, Lilienthal concluded:

Many have departed from their own fields of competence with a cocksure confidence that they can find answers—out of their scientific or technical knowledge or intuition—to what cannot be finally and firmly answered at all: the unimaginably complex and shifting *human* problems involved in the threat of nuclear warfare.

Scientists are human beings. They have shown us that they can be just as wise and just as foolish, just as judicious and just as ridiculous, just as clear-headed and just as bone-headed, as any of us laymen can ever be.[25]

While it is undoubtedly true that the scientist's analytical training does give him a certain advantage over the layman in the vast task of untangling the logic of public controversy, it is easy to give the scientist too much credibility simply because he is a scientist.

The scientific image is often much more attractive than the scientific attitude. Those who claim omnipotence are likely to attract more public attention than those who only form tentative, limited conclusions after careful research and testing. The responsible advocate must seek evidence which reflects the scientific attitude, even if it means his task of supporting his conclusions is made more difficult. Evidence which is the product of the scientific attitude is most dependably found in the more respected journals and books of the various disciplines. It can be found much less dependably in the columns of newspapers and popular and semi-popular magazines. The popularizer has much less of a stake in being accurate than does the scientist, and he realizes the greater difficulties in determining his accuracy. The popularizer often veils his method behind a glib flow of stylized prose, whereas in most scientific journals the evidence and procedures are usually carefully described. It is easier, of course, to understand the non-original scientific writing, but the advocate, if he is to narrow the gap between the two cultures, must strive to achieve the ability to understand the original.

The difficulties of the user of scientific evidence have not ended once he has reached original sources. Care must then be taken to ensure that the evidence is interpreted accurately.

One of the most frequent errors, even committed by scientists themselves, is the failure to follow the rule: *Scientific evidence should not be overgeneralized beyond the bounds of applicability*. The scientist-advocate must make no unwarranted generalizations, from "basic principles" to applied particularizations, or from one application to another quite different application. A variety of psychological experiments with both human beings and animals has established a general principle that reward is *usually* superior to equivalent amounts of punishment in changing behavior.

This basic finding, though frequently true, cannot, however, be applied to an argument for more lenient treatment of prisoners without additional evidence indicating that what is *usually* true *is* true in the specific case of prison inmates.

A second rule pertaining to the interpretation of scientific evidence, and another frequently violated, is: *The advocate must always be aware of the measuring scales he is using.* The physical sciences are full of a multitude of measuring systems which can very easily confuse the novice. It is very easy and quite common to compare two quantities using two very different units of measure, though assuming or claiming that they are the same. Megatons are not kilotons; watts are not amps; micro-curies are not milli-curies. An advocate who claims that an American rocket is better than a Soviet rocket because it has "more power," could be using any of five or six different criteria: pounds thrust, kilograms thrust, horsepower, payload in orbit, payload to target, etc. If he were to use one standard, such as pounds, for the American rocket, and another standard, such as kilograms, for the Soviet, his conclusion would be doubtful at best.

Evidence Must Not Be Attributed to the Discipline as a Whole When It Applies Only to One Investigator. If one worker in a field has reached a conclusion about genetics, this by no means automatically indicates that, "The science of genetics has found. . . ." The formative stages of a scientific investigation are highly controversial. It often takes many years for a discipline to form an undivided judgment on a matter, and on some matters the discipline may never have unified opinion.

Evidence Must Not Be Outdated. Even basic laws and theories are occasionally radically modified, the effect of Einstein's mathematical formulations on Newtonian physics being a case in point. Applied technologies, moreover, change more quickly than any other single area of endeavor. Radar systems used to be "absolutely limited" to a maximum range of several hundred miles. Now new methods of ionospheric and "scatter" propagation have made them capable of seeing many thousands of miles.

Evidence from the *behavioral sciences* deserves special consideration because of its extreme relevance to the material of public controversy. There exist certain very real difficulties to the building of a science of human behavior. The world of man is not nearly so unitary and easy to measure as is the world of physical or biological science. Lord Blackett, head of England's wartime operations research establishment, described the difference as being that "in physical sciences such as physics a great deal of numerical data is ascertainable about relatively simple phenomena," whereas in the behavioral sciences "a limited amount of numerical data is ascertainable about phenomena of great complexity."[26]

The behavioral scientist has attempted to handle the problem of complexity through two divergent methods— either through drawing broad, approximate generalizations or through concentrating on small samples of behavior and making more precise, if limited, judgments. The intent in the latter case has been to eventually combine these small bits of human behavior into a unified theory which could then be used to make more accurate general judgments. At the moment, unfortunately, there is no such unified theory of human behavior resulting from this approach. The task of achieving unity is enormously complicated, and success, if it comes at all, will not come soon. The advocate is thus left with the paradox of a science in which information can be either of general utility or of high accuracy, but rarely both.[27]

The most all-surveying approach to behavior is the *observational,* or *clinical,* method, which has been employed primarily by anthropology, psychiatry, clinical psychology, and, to some extent, sociology. Usually the method consists simply of observation of samples of human behavior, the taking of careful, detailed records, and the use of those records to form the same tentative, limited conclusions which all scientists allow themselves to make. Many broadly applicable theories of behavior have been derived by this means, among them included the Freudian theory of psychosexual development, the psychological-sociological theories of Erich Fromm, and the cross-culture conclusions of Mead, Malinowski, Benedict, and others. Unfortunately findings obtained by the observational method often disagree, a great deal of the disagreement stemming from the absence of systems of measurement of sufficient clarity.

The *correlational,* or *test,* approach to behavior represents an attempt at making measuring systems more accurate. A common form of this method is the questionnaire, which consists of a series of questions which a respondent answers by checking some category such as "yes," "no," "strongly agree," "disagree," or some other appropriate response. The survey itself is a measuring scale. It can be examined by many researchers and is common to all. Results from it can thus be checked and rechecked by others. The survey can, moreover, in some circumstances be more precise because it enables the results to be converted to numbers which can be more exact indicators of attitude and degree. There are several difficulties, however, which an example should help clarify.

Let us say we want to find out about the relationship between anxiety and problem-solving ability. We could obtain a *partial* answer to the question by going out into the field and giving two questionnaires to an average or random sample of people. One would measure their conscious anxiety; the other would measure their problem-solving skill at the moment. The correlational relationship that is obtained through a comparison of the results from the two tests would undoubtedly be complex, but it is probable that we would discover that those people displaying the most anxiety did the poorest on the problem-solving test. There would be, in short, a negative correlation between problem-solving ability and high degrees of anxiety. But this coincidence between anxiety and problem solving does not answer the questions of cause. And this difficulty appears to be an important one associated with the correlational method; the method does not easily discriminate between alternate conditions of causation.

In the above example there are no less than four possibilities with respect to cause:

1. Anxiety causes a person's problem-solving ability to deteriorate.
2. People who possess poor problem-solving ability manage more frequently to involve themselves in anxiety-producing situations, i.e., problem-solving difficulty causes anxiety.
3. Neither factor causes the other to occur. A third factor causes each to happen simultaneously.
4. There are no causal relationships. The coincidence between anxiety and poor problem-solving ability is due entirely to chance.

The last relationship could be almost ruled out by means of statistics which estimate chance. The first three cannot be ruled out by the correlational method, though certain checks can be made to minimize the danger of a misjudgment. The only really positive way of determining causal relationship is to use yet another method which is even more limited in generality of application—the *experimental approach*.

Through the experimental approach the problem set forth in the third factor is almost entirely eliminated by creating a simplified, artificial environment in which all apparently important factors are controlled as much as possible. An understanding of the experimental approach can perhaps be obtained by transferring the example discussed above to an experimental situation. In such a situation if we wanted to find out about the relationship between anxiety and problem solving, we would not go out into the field, but, rather, bring the field into us. A typical segment of the population would be brought to a simple, uniform, artificial environment, perhaps a psychological laboratory. There they would be divided into two groups, an experimental group and a control group, matched as to problem-solving ability by either test or random shuffling. Each group would then be exposed to an identical, controlled environment except in terms of one variable—anxiety. The anxiety stimulus, in whatever form, would be given to the experimental group but not the control group. The responses of both groups would be observed and recorded accurately. If the statistical measurements, based on observations and testing, indicate that the experimental group becomes less able to solve problems as a result of the introduction of anxiety, then the experimenter could non-ambiguously infer that anxiety causes problem-solving difficulty. If no differences in problem solving exist between the two groups, one could then rule out the conclusion that "anxiety causes poor problem-solving ability." (The remaining two possibilities of cause would still have to be verified by means of additional experiments.)

The observational, correlational, and experimental methods each have an important place in the behavioral sciences and in producing evidence of significance to the advocate. The experimental method is often highly accurate, but also very limited, since no one can duplicate a person's life in a laboratory. The observational method at least permits tentative judgments to be made concerning the effect of a person's past behavior and environment on his present behavior and personality. The correlational method, as we have observed, presents problems of both causation and use of statistical analysis.

A final word should be added about statistical analysis, the general technique used most frequently in the behavioral sciences. Statistics are often needed to measure whether an observed or obtained coincidence in behavior was due to "chance" or due to "clearly definable cause." An additional frequent application is that of determining whether a sample of people being tested is large enough and representative enough to be typical of a larger group, perhaps the entire population. Public opinion polls depend on statistical analysis for their validity, and although most of them are now accurate to within several percentage points, there have in the past been notable failures in prediction; these failures have usually been due to an inadequate or non-random sampling. The advocate, in his use of survey and opinion-polling evidence should be aware of the statistical analysis employed, both in terms of the adequacy of the sampling (total number sampled) and its representative nature. A leading worker in the field, Leon Festinger, has warned that a statistical check "when applied, may be anything from a relatively good approximation to a grossly erroneous instrument."[28]

The behavioral sciences are not perfect, but this does not mean they should be ignored. Just as the physical and biological sciences are ignored by the advocate seeking evidence, so are the behavioral sciences. Many state legislatures have repeatedly voted against temporary or permanent suspension of capital punishment, despite consistent testimony from criminologists to the effect that there is little evidence that capital punishment is a significant deterrent to crime.

Evidence from the behavioral sciences, however, has begun to be used in some courts of opinion. As was noted in the previous chapter, the Supreme Court considered predominately correlational evidence obtained from social psychology and found that evidence credible enough to be used as a basis for its historic decision on school segregation in 1954. After reading testimony from sociologist Gunnar Myrdal and social-psychologist Theodore Brameld (among others) as to the finding of thwarted intellectual development of colored children in the South (material given to the court on appellate review), the Court unanimously voted to end the separation of races in American education. Behavioral science for the first time in a constitutional case was allowed to provide factual material on the basis of which the Court might draw legal conclusions.[29]

There is little doubt as to the pressing need for evidence from both the behavioral and the physical-biological sciences in a great many areas of advocacy.

JOURNALISTIC EVIDENCE

Undoubtedly the greatest and most frequented source of evidence in a free society is journalistic evidence, evidence from "the press." The press consists of daily and weekly newspapers, radio and television news and special events, magazines and periodicals, and so-called journalistic books, pamphlets, and tracts on contemporary history and politics, e.g., Victor Lasky's *J.F.K.: The Man and the Myth,* Earl Mazo's *Richard Nixon.* Through the mass media vast amounts of information are made available to the public on almost every public issue. To an uncommon degree the citizen depends on the nation's press to educate him on public controversies and to assist him in forming his opinions on those controversies.

In its simplest form the press observes raw news and information, interprets them by giving them meaning and associating them with certain issues, and communicates its interpretation to the public. The public, in turn, uses the information gained from the press as evidence by which propositions are recognized and positions on the propositions are supported. There is perhaps no greater molder of public opinion than the press, and the advocate confronts journalistic evidence with greater frequency than any other type, employing that evidence constantly either through formulating his own conclusions or through evaluating the conclusions of others. That he needs to have a working knowledge of the nature of journalistic evidence seems self-evident. Two observations should serve to support this assertion.

One observation pertains to the extensiveness of evidence

from the press. The American system of disseminating and collecting news is something to be both admired and feared. If Willie Mays hits a home run in the ninth inning or a little old lady wins a thousand dollars betting on a horse in New Jersey, the information is on the teletype immediately. An earthquake in Chile or a riot in Laos will be reported to the American public within the hour. There is scarcely anything of reasonable interest and/or importance not reported by the American press. Day and night teletype machines spread the news at the rate of over half a million words each twenty-four hours. Almost 1,800 newspapers carry millions of words each day to American homes. Almost 8,000 magazines and periodicals disseminate news and features on the news daily, weekly, monthly, and quarterly, accounting for an aggregate circulation of 384,628,482 copies per issue. More than 3,500 radio stations and 700 television stations beam news and special events daily through 150 million radio sets and 90 million television receivers.[30]

A second observation concerns the impact of this staggering amount of information. That American public opinion today is probably a chief force in the world in terms of its impact on events is a truism. Almost equally accepted is the fact that the American press contributes significantly to the formation of that public opinion through its presentation of news and editorial views.[31]

Because of its accessibility and its extensiveness and because of the regard Americans have long had for the authority of the printed word, evidence from the press has come to assume an almost reverent role in society. News and much editorial comment are often regarded as inviolable and unimpeachable. The phrases "I read in the paper," "Dave Brinkley said," and "*Time* magazine reported that" have too often come to be phrases that end argument, not initiate or prove it. Information from the press is too often accepted and used as highly probative evidence by large numbers of people who fail to attempt in any serious way to sift and evaluate journalistic evidence and to apply to it certain tests of verification in order to ascertain whether indeed it is authentic and reliable, much less applicable to a given argument. Such blind acceptance of evidence can be as much a peril to rational decision-making as the acceptance of hearsay evidence by the attorney or the acceptance without examination of a forgery by an historian, or the belief in an unproved hypothesis by the scientist. The advocate must study journalistic evidence as rigorously, perhaps more so because of the fact that the reporter works under pressures the historian, scientist, and attorney do not have, as any other form of evidence. He must summon each piece of news and editorial comment for cross-examination, assuming each to be possibly fraudulent until proved otherwise.

There are criteria or questions which the advocate should employ in his evaluation of evidence from the press. They apply equally to all forms of journalistic evidence. The basic credibility and trustworthiness of both news interpretation and editorial comment will depend to large degree on the extent to which they meet the demands of the criteria. The criteria actually represent limitations that should be taken into consideration in approaching both the "fact" and "opinion" of journalistic evidence.

1 / *Problems Relating to the Selection and Interpretation of News*

On the occasion of his seventieth birthday, Walter Lippmann, for four decades recognized as one of America's first-rate reporters and pundits, made the following observations concerning the selection and treatment of raw news:

The raw news as such, except when it has some direct and concrete personal or local significance, is to the newspaper readers for the most part inedible and indigestible. The raw news has, therefore, to be processed in order to make it intelligible, for if it is not intelligible, it will not be interesting. And if it is not interesting, it will not be read.

The newspaper correspondents . . . have learned from practical experience that the old rule of thumb about reporters and editorial writers, about news and comment does not fit. . . .

The old rule is that reporters collect the news, which consists of facts, and that the editorial page then utters opinions approving or disapproving of these facts.

It is all very well to say that a reporter collects the news and that the news consists of facts. The truth is that in our world the facts are infinitely many, and that no reporter can collect them all, and that no newspaper could print them all . . . and nobody could read them all.

We have to select some facts rather than others, and in doing that we are using not only our legs but our selective judgment of what is interesting or important or both.

Under these conditions reporting is no longer what we thought of it in much simpler days. If we tried to print only the facts of what had happened—who did what and who said what—the news items would be like the pieces of a jigsaw puzzle thrown in a heap upon the table. The unarranged pieces of raw news would not make a picture at all. Fitting them together so that they do make a picture is the inescapable job of a correspondent.[32]

In short, Lippmann suggests an approach which every advocate should take in considering evidence from the press: The reporter selects from among facts, not *the* facts; he selects facts his judgment tells him are important and interesting. Relevant facts are often unobtainable first-hand, and the reporter must infer them, thus exercising his reasoned judgment. The reporter interprets both his facts and inferences to the public, again in an effort to make them interesting. These opinions alone should demand caution on the part of any advocate approaching journalistic evidence.

2 / Problems Relating to Inaccuracies, Distortions, and Exaggerations

Because so often the reporter must select from among facts, because so often he must infer facts, because so often he must emphasize that which is interesting, and because of the conditions of pressure and chronic obscurity under which he must often work, it is inevitable that inaccuracies, distortions, and exaggerations become integral parts of his product. Anyone who has read Milton Mayer's devastating corrections of a news story in the *Chicago Tribune* could not help but conclude that even "great newspapers" with enormous circulations and first-rate reporters publish articles containing gross numbers of errors and inaccuracies in information.[33] The finding of at least 122 inaccuracies and distortions in one page-one news story of approximately 2,500 words should make any advocate aware of the routine possibilities for error in any news story in any paper. T. S. Matthews, former editor of *Time* magazine, is quoted by Harry Ashmore, former editor of the *Arkansas Gazette,* as reflecting the following commentary on the accuracy of the press:

> When we read the reports on some event we personally know about, we are painfully aware of how wide of the mark we usually are. Every honest editor, and every literate publisher knows that this is so—and those who aren't too tired keep on trying to do something about it.[34]

Nor are newspapers alone the offenders. Critic John Crosby told of an interview with cinemactor Alec Guiness, who had just been the subject of a *Time* magazine cover story. Said Crosby, Guiness exploded with wrath declaring: "It's absolute rubbish, from the cover picture to the story. There are ten, fifteen, or twenty inaccuracies in it. There is no trace of the truth at all. They've even got my son's name and age wrong." Crosby added that other magazines were as guilty as *Time*: "I once spent three days ducking a *Newsweek* researcher . . . because I didn't want to make any statement at all at the moment. But *Newsweek* went right ahead and made up a rather fantastic quote which had me saying a good many things I didn't believe and couldn't possibly have said."[35]

In 1962 historian Arthur Schlesinger discussed the problem at the American Historical Convention in Chicago:

As for newspaper or magazine accounts, they are sometimes worse than useless when they purport to give the inside history of decisions; their relation to reality is often considerably less than the shadows in Plato's cave. I have too often seen the most conscientious reporters attribute to government officials' views the exact opposite of which the officials are advocating within the government to make it possible for me to take the testimony of journalism in such matters seriously again.[36]

The conclusion we wish to draw is not that news and opinion from the press is *generally* inaccurate, but that it can very well be from time to time and that the advocate should accordingly seek to verify the accuracy of whatever journalistic evidence he may wish to use.

In the realm of exaggeration, worth noting is the fact that the press frequently engages in this misdemeanor through substituting a general for a particular statement. The advocate should be aware that the press may term three detectives working on a murder case as "a dragnet hunt," a statement by a New York broker as "Wall Street thinks," or an assertion by a doctor as "medical experts say."

3 / Problems Relating to Bias in the News

Just as the problem of bias or slanting or coloring is of great significance to the historian and the attorney in the evidence they deal with, so does the problem of bias in news reporting exist as one of the major headaches the advocate must deal with in appraising journalistic evidence. Throughout the history of news media, bias in the form of the interpretation of and slanting of facts to fit the special points of view of the press has been a concomitant of news reporting. In the nineteenth century, a "Democratic" newspaper could be depended upon to slant its news according to its preconceptions on issues associated with that news;

a "Republican" newspaper could be depended upon to do likewise. The problem of the distillation of credible facts from obvious biases is, therefore, not a contemporary or unique one in American journalism. The problem has been made more serious, however, by the emergence during the last few decades of what is commonly termed the "one-owner press."

Jefferson's free marketplace of ideas posited a society in which error would be continually offered but would be continually overcome by truth. This marketplace presupposed citizens having access to a variety of sources, each with its point of view, of course, but all of the sources together giving to citizens multiple points of view on any given issue. Through this way evidence offered by one source could be compared to similar evidence offered by numerous other sources; hence verification of credibility would be a matter of reading and analyzing several sources. Until recent years, this concept functioned with some success, most American cities having from half a dozen to a dozen or more newspapers furnishing their readers with varying points of view, and biases, in connection with the evidence on any issue. Today such proliferation no longer exists. As Ashmore points out, we have one-owner press in well over 90 per cent of all American cities and only a handful of publishers putting out weekly or bi-weekly news magazines. The marketplace concept is no longer permitted to work.

Although many journalists have tried to draw general conclusions as to the nature of the biases of the American press, such conclusions have to be taken with some skepticism. Biases vary from publisher to publisher, from publication to publication. Biases may be pro-labor or pro-management, pro-big government, or pro-decentralized government, pro-personal rights or pro-property rights, pro-liberal or pro-conservative. Only through careful reading of both news and editorials and only through knowledge of the behavior and beliefs of the publisher can the advocate determine the type and manner of slanting a publication is apt to engage in.

In what ways does the press bias evidence? The press may, first of all, bias its presentation through the placement and headlining of news. A story on page thirty-six of a newspaper quite obviously has less impact than one on page one. A paper that covered the Kennedy-Nixon campaign in 1960 and that consistently placed stories of the Nixon campaign on page one and stories of the Kennedy campaign on page thirty-six would be demonstrating its strong bias for Nixon. Arthur Rowse, of the *Boston Traveler*, has done a study of press bias as observed in the coverage thirty-one major newspapers gave to the Nixon and Stevenson "fund" stories in the 1952 election campaign. Concerning the placement of news, he observed:

> Only nine of the twenty-eight pro-Eisenhower papers put the Nixon story on the front page at the earliest opportunity; all three of the pro-Stevenson papers did so. And, from that point on, most papers continued to favor one party over the other in the selection, display, and tone of the political news.

Rowse concluded that almost every example of favoritism in the news columns coincided with the paper's editorial feelings, i.e., "papers Republican or Democratic on the editorial page are correspondingly Republican or Democratic in their treatment of the news."[37]

The press often biases evidence through stylistic devices —labeling, name-calling, loaded words, and so on. Thus a "crony" who was a friend of President Truman became a "friend of Presidents" when he associated with President Eisenhower. Student picketers became a "mob of howling, unwashed, bearded beatniks." A Presidential candidate is termed a "scowling, sweaty, uncomfortable politician." A Secretary of State is a "pin-striped cookie-pusher." Reporter Ben E. Bagdikian discussed *Time* magazine's use of style to bias its news reporting:

It is typical of *Time*'s reporting that the political world is generally divided into the forces of evil and the forces of virtue . . . villains "cry"; the heroes "solemnly state." . . . without telling the reader why, the magazine surrounds personalities with an emotional aura, sometimes with adjectives, sometimes with verbs, sometimes with figures of speech. Stylistically, the result is the most dramatic, crisp, and evocative language in the news profession. But politically, it is a vapor of bias that seeps into the text, clouding facts and bypassing the normal critical judgment of the reader.[38]

Time performs the act acutely well but is by no means the only offender. There is scarcely a newspaper or magazine that does not occasionally do the same thing. Witness the Chicago *Tribune* reporting on the 1936 campaign: "Governor Alfred M. Landon tonight brought his great crusade for the preservation of the American form of government into Los Angeles."[39]

Evidence may be biased through communicating it in such a way that people do not perceive its significance or simply failing to communicate it. A most striking example occurred in the 1956 campaign concerning the issue of H-bomb test suspension. The complexity of the issue may have led to newspaper reluctance to deal with it, but more likely the press followed President Eisenhower's views that the issue was not one for public discussion. As a result, press coverage of the issue was little, inadequate, and garbled, making it virtually impossible for citizens to become knowledgeable on the issue, much less perceive its significance. As late as 1959 the science editor of the *New York Herald Tribune*, Earl Ubell, complained that surveys showed that at least one third of the American people had never heard of radioactive fallout and that only 12 per cent of the population knew "technically" what fallout was. Seemingly bias was at work in the press to limit knowledge on the subject.

Finally, a publication may bias the news through space

and time emphasis, i.e., the extensiveness given an event or a person, plus the repetition of stories on the event or person. It may also bias the news through simple avoidance of an issue, an event, or a person. The methods through which the press can focus attention on an issue or a personality are all too obvious, e.g., there is considerable doubt that Senator Joseph McCarthy and the issues he created would ever have been a potent force had the press denied him unjustified coverage. The avoidance of issues and personalities is a method less noticed but equally significant. There are certain so-called untouchable issues the nation's press will ordinarily avoid, thus in effect presenting a biased picture in behalf of the *status quo*. The fear of alienating certain ethnic, religious, patriotic, or economic groups accounts for a good deal of the avoidance. Political motivation, as seen in the case of the debate over H-bomb testing in 1956 constitutes another reason. Few publications, for example, are willing to devote much consideration to the population explosion, because the problem is directly associated with the taboo subject of birth control. When the Legion of Decency attempted to impose a ban on the movie "Baby Doll" in New York City only a few years ago, New York newspapers were almost speechless, avoiding the issue because of its religious implications. Ironically enough, however, Roman Catholics debated the issue with great freedom in their publications.

4 / *Problems Relating to the Manufacturing of News*

In January of 1959 Secretary of State John Foster Dulles devoted much of a press conference to a discussion of the problem of German reunification. He characterized the latest Russian proposals for reunification as "brutal" and "stupid" and emphasized over and over again the inflexibility of the American position, reunification only through free elections. Late in the conference reporter Arthur Sylvester asked the Secretary: ". . . is it our position that free elections are the only method of reuniting Germany? In other words, do we say, 'no free elections, no reunification?'" Dulles' answer seemed to represent an attempt to avoid the appearance of keeping his mind closed to new avenues toward peace: ". . . we never have said that. The formula of reunification by free elections was the agreed formula. . . . But I wouldn't say that it is the only method by which reunification could be accomplished." This statement, which was a logical answer to an "or else" question, was presented by much of the press as one suggesting an important change in American policy. Most papers reacted similarly to the *New York Times,* whose lead article the following morning began: "Secretary of State Dulles said today the United States and its allies were trying to find new proposals for solving the problem of Germany." The world repercussions were immediate and loud. Britain was "disturbed"; the French "upset"; and West Germany "shocked." Even the careful explanations of President Eisenhower and Secretary Dulles did not assuage the feelings of America's allies. The press, as one newspaper put it, "had created a fantasy which had reverberated 'round the world.'"[40]

5 / *Problems Relating to News Management*

Up to now in discussing problems associated with the credibility of journalistic evidence, we have addressed ourselves primarily to the treatment of the news by the press itself. There are, however, difficulties involved in the finding and presentation of journalistic evidence that are beyond the control of the profession itself at times. A great percentage of vital news comes from government, particularly the Federal government. Through various devices the government can exert strong control over the news; the government can "manage" the news, allowing the press only that evidence the government thinks the press should have (in the interests of "security" or self-interest) or coloring or slanting the news to make it fit more closely whatever images of its activities the government wishes to emphasize at a given time. *New York Times* columnist James Reston coined the phrase "the management of news" to describe any governmental policy of issuing false evidence, suppressing evidence, distorting evidence, or harassing unfriendly critics. In his testimony in front of Representative John E. Moss' committee investigating the availability of information from Federal departments and agencies (in March, 1959), Reston voiced his apprehensions:

Most of my colleagues here have been talking primarily about the suppression of news. I would like to direct the committee to an important aspect of this problem which I think is the growing tendency to manage the news. Let me see if I can illustrate what I mean:

I think there was a conscious effort to give the news at the Geneva Conference (in 1955) an optimistic flavor. I think there was a conscious effort there, decided upon even perhaps ahead of time, for spokesmen to emphasize all the optimistic facts coming out of that conference and to minimize all of the quarrels at that conference. . . .

After the Geneva Conference a decision was taken in the government that perhaps this was having a bad effect, that the people in the Western countries were letting down their guard, and therefore a decision was made . . . that the government should strike another note. So that after the Geneva smiling, the new word went out that it might be a good idea now to frown a little bit, so the President made a speech at Philadelphia, taking quite a different light about the Geneva Conference. That is what I mean by managing the news.

Reston's observations were more than a year before the now famous U-2 incident of May, 1960, in which the Federal government first lied about the fact that an American plane had been downed while spying over Russia and then blurted out the truth, which was that we had been spying this way for years. Reston's observations were made more than three years prior to the mysterious mid-October days of 1962, during which the government either lied about an evolving critical situation in Cuba (the Pentagon disclaimed any knowledge of offensive missiles in Cuba) or the government simply suppressed all news about any possibility of Russian missiles in Cuba. In both the U-2 incident and the Cuban missile crisis the government "managed" the news, the very type of problem Reston was concerned with in March, 1959, depriving the press of its evidence and hence the American people of their right to know.

Of course "managed news" was not a problem of only the Eisenhower and Kennedy administrations. George Washington warned delegates to the Constitutional Convention to avoid reporters. Abraham Lincoln suppressed the Emancipation Proclamation for three months because his advisers feared its release might cost the Republican Party an election. Franklin Roosevelt was a master, as many have testified, at controlling news. But in an era in which many decisions are those affecting life or death, an evidence-seeking public has less toleration for any situation which seeks to limit or distort news. Nor is the concern confined to the general public. Senator Hubert Humphrey complained during the last years of the Eisenhower administration that, "On many aspects of our national security the information that is necessary to have before making decisions and rendering judgments is not even available to the Congress, much less the public." Humphrey asserted that in his work with the Senate Subcommittee on Disarmament and its investigation of measures necessary to discontinue nuclear weapons development, "it took us literally months to find people in the executive branch . . . who were willing and prepared to discuss the problem of the detection of nuclear weapons test, and even when we found them the administration refused to allow many of them to testify under the rights of executive privilege." Humphrey asked the question many advocates ask: "How could we possibly make the decisions we needed to make when evidence was suppressed?"[41]

Hanson W. Baldwin, military analyst for the *New York Times,* addressed his thoughts to problems of management and secrecy in an article in *Atlantic Monthly.* The last two decades, he said, had seen enormous growth of governmental secrecy, a growth influenced by the ever-increasing Federal police power (the F.B.I. and the Central Intelligence Agency), and of the "intelligence mentality," which tends to enshrine secrecy as an abstract good. Such factors have led to a "wall of secrecy" which has gradually been built around government. The advocate might well agree with Mr. Baldwin's conclusion: "No people can be really free if its press is spoonfed with government pap or if the news which provides a democracy with the rationale for its actions is so controlled, restricted, managed, or censored that it cannot be published."[42]

What conclusions might the advocate draw from this discussion of journalistic evidence, conclusions relevant to his purpose? Since much of the unfortunately bad evidence used in advocacy tends to be of the journalistic variety, the advocate must use great caution in the evaluation and use of such evidence. He must approach all evidence from journalism with the realization that such material represents the judgment and interpretation of a reporter who often works in an atmosphere of "chronic obscurity." The advocate must understand that inaccuracies and distortions are an inherent aspect of journalism, in spite of the diligent efforts, at times, of the press to prevent such errors. He must accept the fact that bias and coloring enter into almost any piece of news, that news is often manufactured by the reporter and the news media and therefore may bear little direct association with the actual event. And the advocate must know that attempts to manage news often result in inadequate or slanted information. With an understanding of these problems the advocate in dealing with journalistic evidence should be better able to select his evidence more wisely and verify that evidence as much as possible before he employs it.

►NOTES◄

1. H. L. Mencken, *Prejudices* (New York: Vintage Books, 1958), 242 ff.
2. Barnet Baskerville, "The Illusion of Proof," *Western Speech* (Fall, 1961), pp. 236-240.
3. Charles M. Solley and Gardner Murphy, *Development of the Perceptual World* (New York: Basic Books, Inc., 1960).
4. See S. I. Hayakawa, *Language in Thought and Action* (New York: Harcourt, Brace & World, Inc., 1964); Irving J. Lee, *Language Habits in Human Affairs* (New York: Harper & Row, Publishers, 1941); Wendell Johnson, *People in Quandaries* (New York: Harper & Row, Publishers, 1946).
5. Arthur M. Schlesinger, Jr., "The Historian as Artist," *Atlantic Monthly* (June, 1963), p. 35.
6. Arthur M. Schlesinger, Jr., "The Historian and History," *Foreign Affairs* (April, 1963), p. 493.
7. Louis Gottschalk, "The Historian and the Historical Document," in *The Use of Personal Documents in History, Anthropology and Sociology* (New York: Social Science Research Council, 1946), p. 8.
8. Alan Nevins, *The Gateway to History* (Garden City, N. Y.: Anchor Books, 1962), p. 180.
9. Gottschalk, *op. cit.*, p. 16.
10. Nevins, *op. cit.*, p. 198.
11. Gottschalk, *op. cit.*, p. 41.
12. Gottschalk, *ibid.*, p. 45.
13. Gottschalk, *ibid.*
14. See *Atlantic Monthly* (April, 1929), pp. 516-525.
15. Gottschalk, *op. cit.*, p. 35.
16. Nevins, *op. cit.*, p. 225.
17. *Commentaries III* (New York: Harper & Bros., 1858), p. 367.
18. James B. Thayer, *Preliminary Treatise on Evidence*, (n.p.), 1898, p. 2.
19. John H. Wigmore, *Treatise on Evidence* (Boston: Little, Brown and Company, 1904), Vol. I, p. 13.

20. Thomas Starkie, *Evidence*, 1824, Vol. I, p. 13.

21. Wigmore, *op. cit.*, p. 4.

22. See Charles E. Osgood, "Reciprocal Initiative," in James Roosevelt (ed.), *The Liberal Papers* (Garden City, N. Y.: Doubleday & Company, Inc., 1962), pp. 155-229.

23. Gerald Holton, "The False Images of Science," in Richard Thruelsen and John Kobler (eds.), *Adventures of the Mind* (New York: Alfred A. Knopf, Inc., 1961), pp. 511-529.

24. C. P. Snow, *The Two Cultures and the Scientific Revolution* (New York: Cambridge University Press, 1960), pp. 53-54.

25. *New York Times Western Edition* (September 30, 1963), p. 9. Also in Mr. Lilienthal's book, *Change Hope, and the Bomb* (Princeton, N. J.: Princeton University Press, 1963).

26. Lord Blacket, "Operations Research," *Advance of Science* (April, 1948), p. 29.

27. The closest approach to a unified theory is represented in the work done by Skinner, Dollard, Miller, *et al,* relating to a stimulus-response theory. Currently the theory is hardly all-inclusive in character, though it is gaining acceptance rapidly. There is some doubt that it will soon gain the status of generality of theories arrived at by means of the observational method.

28. Leon Festinger, "Assumptions Underlying the Use of Statistical Techniques," in Marie Jahoda, Morton Deutsch, Stuart Cook (eds.), *Research Methods in Social Relations* (New York: The Dryden Press, Inc., 1951), Vol. II, p. 716.

29. See text of decision in *U. S. Reports* (347 US 483 1954). See also James Reston, "A Sociological Decision," *New York Times* (May 18, 1954), p. 14.

30. Statistics as of 1960; see Richard Chapin, *Mass Communications: A Statistical Analysis* (East Lansing, Mich.: Michigan State University Press, 1959).

31. Among the many writers who discuss the impact of the press on public opinion are: Wilbur Schramm, *The Process and Effects of Mass Communication*

(Princeton, N. J.: Princeton University Press, 1954); Richard LaPiere, *Theory of Social Control* (New York: McGraw-Hill Book Company, 1954); Melvin DeFleur and Otto Larsen, *The Flow of Information,* (New York: Harper & Row, Publishers, 1958); Joseph T. Klapper, *The Effects of Mass Communication* (New York: The Free Press of Glencoe, 1960).

32. *Washington Post* (September 24, 1959), p. 16.
33. Milton Mayer, "How to Read the Chicago Tribune," *Harper's Magazine* (April, 1949), pp. 24-35.
34. Harry Ashmore, "Has Our Free Press Failed Us?" *Saturday Evening Post* (October 29, 1960), p. 50.
35. John Crosby, Chicago *Sun-Times* (October 14, 1959), p. 43.
36. Schlesinger, "The Historian and History," *loc. cit.,* p. 493.
37. Arthur Edward Rowse, *Slanted News* (Boston: Beacon Press, 1957).
38. Ben Bagdikian, *Providence Journal* (October 20, 1958).
39. Arthur M. Schlesinger, Jr., *The Politics of Upheaval* (Boston: Houghton-Mifflin Company, 1960), p. 633.
40. For additional information see Douglas Cater, *The Fourth Branch of Government* (Boston: Houghton-Mifflin Company, 1959).
41. Address at Northwestern University, February 7, 1959.
42. Hanson W. Baldwin, "Managed News: Our Peacetime Censorship," *Atlantic Monthly* (April, 1963), pp. 53-59.

► E X E R C I S E S ◄

1. Prepare two five-minute speeches of advocacy on a significant controversy. The first speech should contain arguments unsupported by evidence (so far as possible); the second speech should contain arguments strongly substantiated by a variety of evidence. Your audience can then discuss the persuasiveness of each

speech, noting arguments that were believable without evidence, arguments that were not persuasive without evidence, the nature of the evidence offered in the second speech and why this evidence was or was not probative.

2. Prepare a report on the evidence used by advocates addressing themselves to the following public controversies. Outline the arguments put forth by each advocate and list the evidence presented in support of each argument. Evaluate the quantity and credibility of the evidence.

a. Adlai E. Stevenson, "Cease H-Bomb Testing," *New York Times* (October 16, 1956), p. 18.
Dwight D. Eisenhower, "H-Bomb Proposal 'Pie in the Sky,'" *New York Times* (October 19, 1956), p. 13.

b. Robert M. Hutchins, "The Path to War," *Vital Speeches* (January 23, 1941), Vol. VII, no. 9, pp. 258-261; or "The Proposition is Peace," *Vital Speeches* (March 30, 1941), Vol. VII, no. 13, pp. 389-392.
Franklin D. Roosevelt, "A State of Emergency Exists," *Vital Speeches* (May 27, 1941), Vol. VII, no. 16, pp. 508-512.

c. Eric Larrabee, "Scientists in Collision: Was Velikovsky Right?" *Harper's Magazine* (August, 1963), Vol. CCXXVII, no. 1359, pp. 48-55.
Donald H. Menzel, "The Debate over Velikovsky," *Harper's Magazine* (December, 1963), Vol. CCXXVII, no. 1363, pp. 83-87.

d. Joseph McCarthy, "Stevenson Soft on Communism," *New York Times* (October 28, 1952), p. 26.
Adlai E. Stevenson, "President Yields to McCarthyism," *New York Times* (March 7, 1954), p. 62.

e. Barry Goldwater, "Economic Realities: The Federal Government," *Vital Speeches* (January 15, 1964), Vol. XXX, no. 8, pp. 234-237.

f. Rev. Robert F. Drinan, "State and Federal Aid to Parochial Schools," *Vital Speeches* (July 1, 1964), Vol. XXX, no. 18, pp. 559-562.

    g. Terry Sanford, "By Their Own Free Choice: To-
       bacco and Cancer," *Vital Speeches* (April 16,
       1964) Vol. XXX, no. 15, pp. 463-467.

    h. Max Rafferty, "Today's Challenge in Education,"
       Vital Speeches (February 28, 1963), Vol. XXIX,
       no. 15, pp. 450-454.

3. Present a four-minute speech of advocacy in which
   ample evidence is used to support your proposition.
   After the speech there will be a question period during
   which the rest of the audience attempts to impeach
   your evidence; be ready to defend it.

4. In his book *Debates With Historians* (New York: Meri-
   dian Books, Inc., 1958), professor of history Pieter
   Geyl of the University of Utrecht launched a vigorous
   attack on historian Arnold Toynbee's six-volume *Study
   of History*. Writes Geyl, the Toynbee "system" of interpreting history is not only "useless," but it "revolts
   the scholar in me . . . rouses me to protest." Toynbee's
   prophecy Geyl regards as a "blasphemy against Western civilization."
   Read the three chapters of attack in Geyl's volume—
   Chapters V, VII, and VIII. Observe his use of historical
   evidence in both the chapters themselves and the documentation to the chapters. Appraise and evaluate Geyl's
   evidence in terms of this chapter's discussion of historical evidence. How convincing is his use of evidence?
   List Geyl's "arguments" and then determine to what
   extent each argument is supported by evidence.

5. Assistant Secretary of Defense Arthur Sylvester became
   a strong advocate of the policy of governmental news
   management during the Kennedy administration. After
   the Cuban missile crisis of 1962 he stated, "News flowing from actions taken by the government is a part of
   the weaponry of the government." At a Sigma Delta
   Chi meeting he stated that a government facing nuclear
   destruction "has the right, if necessary, to lie to save
   itself." As we have observed in this chapter, *New York
   Times* writer Hanson Baldwin takes strong exception to
   Mr. Sylvester's viewpoint, believing that such a policy

prevents people from being really free. Marshal as many arguments as you can to support each point of view; reach a decision of your own and justify that decision.

6. Read Albert Wohlsetter's article, "Scientists, Seers, and Strategy," in *Foreign Affairs* (April, 1963), Vol. 41, No. 3, pp. 466-479. To what extent, if any, do you agree with Mr. Wohlsetter's criticism of the scientist as a political prophet?

▶ 5 ◀ PROOF THROUGH REASONING

In the investigation of a problem, conclusions must be inferred, and in advocacy, conclusions must be proved. This chapter will explain the processes of reasoning which link evidence with conclusions; it will describe how conclusions are inferred and proved. We will define a reasoning process as the relationship between evidence and a conclusion. This chapter will describe those patterns of reasoning which are most frequently used in argumentation and which the advocate will find of most use in supporting his conclusions.

The total unit of proof is an argument. This has traditionally been defined as a statement (conclusion) which follows from other statements (premises), but this definition is not precise enough, since there are three functional elements in an argument. These are the evidence, the conclusion, and the warrant. The *evidence* consists of facts, data, opinions, or other kinds of information. *Conclusions* may be of many types. They may make a general assertion, such as "teachers are paid low salaries"; they may assert a value judgment, as "advertising is beneficial to the nation"; they may assert a fact, as "country X is preparing to invade country Y." Their common characteristic is that they go beyond the evidence in making an assertion, but the assertion claims to follow from the evidence. The third element in an argument is the *warrant*. This is a general principle which says that the conclusion may be drawn from the evidence, i.e., it tells why the conclusion follows from the evidence. A diagram will illustrate the relationships:

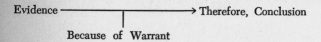

Evidence ————————————→ Therefore, Conclusion

Because of Warrant

Let us take a sample argument and separate it into the three elements:

> Recent news reports from Dullnia say the government is considering buying corn on the world market. U. S. officials say this means that the corn crop is failing this year, since otherwise there would be no reason for Dullnia to buy corn.

Evidence: Dullnia is pur- ————————→ Therefore, *conclusion*:
chasing corn on the world   Dullnia's corn crop is fail-
market.   ing.

Because of the *warrant*:
If a country buys corn on
the world market, then,
usually, its own crop is
failing.

If the warrant is granted, then the conclusion follows from the evidence, but if the warrant is not acceptable, then the argument is not probable. The warrant in this case is a general principle, probably derived from historical observation, and it is one which holds for all similar situations. The analysis of this argument brings us to three important observations: (1) The elements in an argument are not always stated explicitly. Often the warrant is assumed or implied, on the assumption that the audience will be aware of the principle and accept it as valid. The above argument would be understood if it were stated: "If Dullnia is considering buying corn on the world market, its domestic crop must be failing." (2) The arguments of the advocate always lead to *probable* conclusions, not certain conclusions. The conclusion of the sample argument is only probable because there could be other reasons for considering the purchase of corn, e.g., a desire to stockpile corn. (3) There may be several sub-arguments in the over-all argument. For example, are the news reports true? And is the corn crop really failing or might it not always be less than adequate? These sub-conclusions might be granted or they might be questioned, depending on the evidence and warrants which support them.[1]

THE PROCESSES OF REASONING

We will now consider the different types of arguments which the advocate uses. There are different types of conclusions which the advocate may support, and there are varying processes which lead from evidence to those conclusions.[2]

1 / Reasoning from Characteristics to a Description (by criteria of definition)

The conclusion of this type of reasoning is that an event should be classified or described with a certain term. Examples of these conclusions are:

China's attack on India was *aggression*.
Juvenile delinquency is a *problem* in X city.
The Tennessee Valley Authority is an *efficient* business.

In each case the point of the argument is that the event should be described in a particular way. For example, the Chinese attack was aggression, not an accident, self-defense, or justifiable claiming of territory. Implicit in the argument is a definition of the term, and the evidence and warrant are concerned with the definition. In effect, the argument must show what we mean by "aggression" and that the event in question fits that definition. The warrant of the argument states the definition of the term in the conclusion. "Aggression" might be defined as "unprovoked attack to obtain control of territory on the part of a nation." We will refer to this definition as "criteria" for the use of the term. Thus the warrant states criteria of definition for when the term may be used and when it may not be used. These criteria are characteristics which the event must have to be described according to the conclusion. If the event has the necessary characteristics, then we apply the descriptive term. Whenever one nation attacks another, without provocation, in an attempt to seize control of the land or government, we refer to the event as "aggression." The evidence for the argument consists of the characteristics of the event which fulfill the criteria.

Let us assume we learn that the Bounce-O Company controls the manufacture of all ping-pong balls in the United States. We would conclude that it is a monopoly, because the criteria for a monopoly are that (1) a firm must have exclusive control of a commodity or service in a particular market or (2) a control that makes possible the manipulation of prices. The characteristics satisfy the first set of criteria, so the firm is a monopoly.

Evidence: Bounce-O Company controls the manufacture of all ping-pong balls in the United States. ⟶ *Conclusion*: Therefore, the Bounce-O Company is a ping-pong ball monopoly.

Warrant: Because companies which have exclusive control of a commodity in a market are called monopolies.

You will note that there are several alternate sets of criteria which lead to "monopoly," but the warrant need state only the one which applies to this particular situation. Often there will be several types of circumstances which can be described by the same term. For example, in establishing that a situation is a "problem," these criteria are all possible: a situation which is a source of danger, suffering, or degradation to those who experience it; a situation which prevents the operation of and growth toward an ideal; a situation which makes our society or the institutions in it operate less effectively than they should; etc.

This same process of reasoning may be used to demonstrate that a situation does not fit the criteria for a certain classification:

> We contend that Congress is not representative of the people. If a representative policy means that it is made by a majority of the people through their congressmen, then this is not the case with Congress. Let's look at some statistics. Two-fifths of the population elect three-fifths of the representatives to the House, and the majority of the senators are elected by only 19 per cent of the population.

In analyzing arguments based on this process of reasoning, attention should focus on the warrant and the evidence. The argument in actual use may not make the warrant explicit, and in this case it must be inferred from the definition of the conclusion and the characteristics cited. (Specifically, you should infer what the advocate assumed the criteria to be from the characteristics he cites as evidence, then compare these inferred criteria with the criteria which you believe are most adequate for the definition of the conclusion.) First, the criteria in the warrant should be evaluated carefully to determine if they are a satisfactory definition for the conclusion. Are any additional criteria necessary for the definition? And would there be any exceptions or qualifications in classifying an event on the basis of the criteria? If the criteria given or inferred are not adequate for a good definition of the conclusion, then the argument is not a probative one.

Second, the evidence must be examined to determine if it satisfies the criteria, whether expressed or implicit. The company must control all the product, not 51 per cent of the market; a situation must cause suffering unjustifiably, etc. Here is an example in which the characteristics do not satisfy the criteria which are required by the conclusion:

> In the state of New York there is continual misadministration of the unemployment compensation money. Last year over 40 per cent of the claims filed were fraudulent, and 20 per cent of the payments went to persons who were not legally entitled to them.

The conclusion, in the first sentence, applies the description "misadministration" to the evidence, but the evidence does not satisfy the criteria for misadministration. Fraudulent claims may be filed and persons receive money which they are not entitled to without the situation being one of misadministration. Before misadministration can be said to exist, the officials must deliberately use money in ways not intended or authorized, and such is not the case. In addition to this, the conclusion asserts that the situation is "continual," and to satisfy the criteria of definition for this, the advocate would have to present characteristics of regular recurrence of the situation.

2 / Reasoning from Characteristics to a Value Judgment (by criteria of value)

At some point in his analysis the investigator must assign values to the events which he studies. A newspaper is judged a good newspaper; a policy is concluded to be harmful; Federal aid to education is decried as evil, or proclaimed as good; racial discrimination is claimed unjust. All of these conclusions make a value judgment about the evidence, a statement which can be translated into terms of good and bad or located on a scale of merit. The claims are not all related to the same field of values. The scale may be for newspapers, for people, for social situations, for Christian or Moslem cultures, but all are recognizable as value statements, dependent not upon sense observation, but upon value and preference systems held by the individual and by society.

Evidence: Newspaper X ⟶ *Conclusion*: Therefore, has thoughtful editorials, newspaper X is a good accurate and comprehensive reporting, and good typography.

Warrant: Because a good newspaper satisfies the criteria of having good editorial writing, accurate and comprehensive reporting, and good physical composition.

This value judgment is assigned on the basis of characteristics of the event (the newspaper), and any newspaper with those characteristics would satisfy the criteria of value. Another type of value argument assigns value to an event because of its effects or consequences.

Evidence: Liberalizing di- ⟶ *Conclusion*: Liberalizing vorce laws would make divorce laws would be marriages less stable. bad.

Warrant: Anything which contributes to instability in marriage is bad.

The evidence for conclusions of value describes factual events: characteristics or consequences of a situation. The conclusion makes a value judgment about the data, assigning it a position on a good-bad scale. The warrant is a direct statement that certain circumstances are good or bad, wise or unwise, just or unjust, and to what degree. In investigating an argument, the advocate should go past the immediate warrant to discover why the value is assigned, i.e., what basic values are present and what value system they belong to. In the argument on the inadvisability of liberalizing divorce laws, the warrant says that "marriage instability" is bad. This assignment of value could be supported by indicating the bad consequences resulting from instability in marriage, e.g., lack of security, effect on children, economic disruption, etc. The values assigned to these events can be backed by their contribution to the perpetuation of the community itself. And the importance of the community can be based on other values.

We point out that this is not the only line of argument which may ultimately claim that easy divorce is a bad thing. There may be values based on fair play, justice, human dignity, theological or religious values, or tradition. The process of reasoning and the method of analysis would still be the same. And the same would be true of an argument supporting the opposite position.

The warrant will always consist of criteria. The elements stated by the warrant in the newspaper argument are criteria for a good newspaper. (For some a newspaper may be "good" if it supports their political party, but this is another field of values!) The establishment of the evidence will often depend on argument by criteria of definition (By thorough news reporting is meant . . .) and the warrant itself will be supported by standards taken from the field of argument (Accurate news reporting is good journalism because . . .). Some warrants will state criteria of value explicitly (e.g., the newspaper argument), while others will state general classes of events which are assigned value (e.g., the divorce argument). Depending on the warrant it may be necessary for the evidence to satisfy all of the criteria, or on the other hand, there may be alternative sets or combinations or a certain number of criteria to be satisfied, rather than a specific group. Then, too, there are hierarchies of values, and usual standards may be superseded under changed circumstances. For example, courts have ruled that the freedom of speech guaranteed by the First

Amendment to the Constitution may be superseded when such freedom presents clear and present danger to the social order. Here is an assertion that certain values take precedence over other values which in normal times are supreme. However, others have challenged the line of demarcation which some rulings have drawn, saying that the decision encroaches on freedom of speech unjustifiably and that the freedom can be controverted only in extreme circumstances. That these positions are based on values should be obvious.

This leads us to a consideration of value structures themselves. Most of the value judgments in argumentative analysis will be grounded in the immediate field of the argument. In economics there are accepted standards for good investments and sound risks. In political systems there are criteria for wise public policy. In journalism, in rhetoric, in the military, in every field there are criteria of value relative to that field. These systems interlock and overlap, sometimes consistently, sometimes inconsistently, so that any one event, e.g., birth control, may be viewed from the vantage points of more than one set of values and arguments may be constructed on the basis of each system. In addition to these field-dependent values, there are over-all cultural or social values which are relatively (but only that) independent of specific fields of experience and relate to "human experience" or "superhuman experience." The Judeo-Christian heritage is such a value system. These systems are usually concerned with how one interacts with his fellow men and his environment. The structure of the system may be complex and may be inconsistent in places. As with field-dependent systems there will be values which are asserted and acted upon, and there may be values which are asserted but not followed.

An over-all cultural value system obviously overlaps the sub-systems within the society. It may reinforce some of their values but it may also be inconsistent with them. General standards of morality may conflict with specific standards of, say, political morality. When this conflict occurs, either one value may be rejected or minimized or both may be maintained inconsistently. In this latter case individuals may be responsive to arguments from both values, though not simultaneously. Or arguments can be constructed in such a way as to strengthen the response to one of the value assumptions. For example, the practice of capital punishment is obviously inconsistent with the sixth commandment, but many persons firmly believe in both of them. But one might base a strong argument on the latter value, attempting to make it strong enough to overcome the positive value associated with capital punishment.

Because hierarchies of values overlap within a culture and because the basic values of any culture can be challenged by comparison with those of another culture, the analyst may wonder what values he should use in an argumentative investigation of a problem. Actually, the problem of what values to use need not arise very often in argumentation, because the investigator can ground his judgments in the set of values surrounding the problem which he is investigating, or more broadly, in the values which make the situation a problem. This is because a situation can be considered a problem only if it conflicts with or affects certain values of people or society. Therefore, these values usually provide a context for judgments about the events. In reasoning about defamation suits, for example, the fundamental values recognized by the law are the worth of wealth, health, and reputation. In the question of separate versus integrated schools, the Constitution recognizes the value of certain individual rights derived from being human. However, there are undoubtedly cases when two sets of values conflict and one must choose between them. (An oft-repeated conflict is between idealistic and practical values.) What to do? Here we prefer not to advise the advocate. The decision is personal to the investigator and will probably grow out of his own subtle beliefs and feelings about what is right. It is one of the many existential moments which occur when we make decisions.[3]

Nevertheless, we must consider some of the methods for evaluating the process. Because the principle of inference is similar in process to the argument by criteria of definition, the methods of evaluation are also similar. First the criteria of values in the warrant must be made explicit. If the criteria are not stated, they can often be inferred from the evidence of the argument as well as from the advocate's understanding of the values surrounding the field. These value standards should be analyzed to determine their acceptability. Are they an adequate formulation of the factors necessary to assign value in this area? Are there any criteria omitted or are there qualifications on their application? The range of variability within the criteria must also be considered. Is a newspaper good if it has complete and accurate news coverage but mediocre typography? How unchristian is life imprisonment? In most cases the investigator should go beyond the warrant to its backing and even beyond that, until he has a thorough understanding of the values underlying the claim.

Once the criteria are established, the next aspect of evaluation is whether the data satisfy the criteria. The characteristics of the event must fulfill the conditions for the assignment of value, e.g., the news reporting must really be accurate. Here the problem of the range of variability of the criteria arises. The characteristics may be more than adequate in terms of one criterion but less than adequate for another. Which is of more importance depends upon the cultural hierarchy of values.

An important difference must be kept in mind between this argument and argument by criteria of definition. In the process based on definition, the range of alternative definitions is limited: monopoly is a fairly well-defined usage, and a definition of the term is almost interchangeable with the use of the term itself. However, there are many roads which lead to value claims, and different sets of criteria may lead to identical or similar value judgments.

Consider the criteria for judging a college or university to be good. A small, denominational, co-educational college may be judged good for those very reasons, but any one of those criteria may be absent in the characteristics of another school which is also considered good. A good physical plant is a highly valued characteristic, but a university with poor physical facilities may nevertheless be "good" because of other characteristics which satisfy other criteria. Thus, the criteria of value are often not the necessary criteria which the criteria of definition are, and their discovery and application is more subjective.

3 / Reasoning from Example to a Descriptive Generalization

In this process one or more examples are examined and then a generalization is made describing all examples of the same type. The conclusion is not just a description of the examined examples, but applies to examples not observed. Certain characteristics of the evidence are described and the conclusion asserts that all similar events have the same characteristics. "Similar events" means events from the same class, such as liquor stores, Lichtensteineans, libel cases, libraries, or lurid movies. The warrant asserts that the examples in the evidence are typical and their characteristics can be extended over the entire class.

Communist Kilov has always followed the Moscow party policy in his own political assertions. ⟶ All Communists follow the Moscow policy in their personal political assertions.

Communist Slansky has also.

So has Communist Smith.

What is true of Kilov, Slansky, and Smith is true of all Communists because the three are typical members of the party.

The warrant asserts that the example is typical, that is, what is true of it is true of all or of most of the events similar to it. The term "typical" or "representative" is used to indicate the possibility of generalizing. In the following argument, the typicality of the examples is implied rather than stated.

There is a close correlation between the availability of medical services and the income of the people in a particular region. In the state of New York, which has a high per capita income, we find one doctor for every five hundred individuals, while in the state of Mississippi, where the average income is quite low, we find one doctor for every fifteen hundred individuals. We find one nurse for every four hundred twenty persons in New York and one for every twenty-four hundred persons in Mississippi.

There are actually two factors which are generalized in this argument. The first is that the correlation between income and medical services holds true in New York and Mississippi for those medical services not mentioned in the argument, e.g., hospitals, research institutions. The second assumption of generality is that the correlation will hold true for other states.

It is important to understand the various ways that the typicality of the example can be established. There are several methods of doing this:

A. *Sampling and statistical analysis.* Television rating polls, political opinion polls, and public opinion surveys are uses of sampling techniques in which a sample is taken from a larger population and subjected to statistical analysis; the results are then extended to the entire population. The method of selecting the sample is an important factor. A random selection may be made (e.g., every one hundredth name in the phone directory) on the generally reliable assumption that a fairly typical group of individuals (examples) will be discovered. Or a selection may be taken from specific groups within the over-all population. A refined political survey might select laborers, farmers, office workers, and executives and people from urban areas, rural areas, etc., trying to match the over-all makeup of the population. The exact groups selected would depend upon the purpose of the generalization, and each group would be analyzed according to its weight in the over-all group. Statistical analysis can then calculate the reliability of a generalization.[4]

B. *The number of examples.* Usually the more examples that we find which are similar, the more we can assume they are representative of the entire group. In areas where rhetorical discourse is used, in history, political science, economics, etc., one well-analyzed example may be sufficient, or several may add more support, depending on the other factors which we will describe.

C. *The diversity of characteristics in the examples which are not included in the generalization.* If the examples show similarities reported in the generalization but have many other differences, then it is more likely that the generalization will hold true. In a public opinion poll, if 98 per cent of the sample favor a certain policy, even though the individuals come from many various groups—political, economic, social, educational—then this indicates that the factor is relatively independent of other characteristics and can be more safely generalized.

D. *The similarity of causes producing the characteristics.* The characteristics described in the generalization can be traced to causes or conditions. If these causal factors are common to the class from which the examples come, the warrant is strengthened.

4 / Reasoning from Example to a Causal Generalization

This argument asserts that certain events are usually followed by other events: *x* causes *y;* public schools promote democratic attitudes; logical arguments produce more change of opinion with intelligent people than with un-intelligent people. Separate facilities for white and Negro students result in poorer education for Negro students; the dirty words in dictionaries corrupt our youth. As in a descriptive generalization, the conclusion describes a selected aspect of the examples and asserts that it applies to all examples or events of the same type, but the causal generalization asserts a causal, sequential relation rather than a co-existent pattern of characteristics. The evidence of the argument is usually examples or events or situations which exhibit this causal relation.[5] However, some causal arguments are built up from chains of arguments, and examples are not the immediate data but are back in the chain. Consider this series of arguments leading to the final claim that segregated schools cause poorer education for the Negro students. (See the diagram on p. 172.) What seems to be a simple claim can be analyzed into a chain of sub-arguments, eventually grounded in examples but mediated by intervening causal generalizations.

The examples which are evidence for causal conclusions must satisfy the same requirements for typicality as those for descriptive conclusions. That is, we must show that the description of the causal relation can be extended as a general principle. The methods for confirming generality which we discussed for descriptive generalizations—unbiased selection, number, irrelevant characteristics, and underlying causes—are equally applicable for causal generalizations. Besides these principles, we can add some more subjective methods of judging the generality of the principle in the data. If we know something about the general class, we may draw on our experience, knowledge, and reasoning about the subject. We may "intuitively" feel that these examples are representative and the principles true on a non-conscious level of awareness. This is not supposed to sound mysterious. It is just that we *can* make judgments on the basis of many factors which are so subtle and complex that they cannot be verbalized. A second reason we

Segregation in schools is on the basis of color. ⟶ In segregated schools Negro students have inferiority feelings. ⟶ In segregated schools Negro students' learning is interfered with.

Segregation on the basis of color causes feelings of inferiority.

Inferiority feelings interfere with learning.

may consider examples typical is that we recognize that the principles and relationships would be true of any other examples of the type. In science, for example, one or two experiments will usually suffice to demonstrate a principle, because natural laws are the same in any experiment. A third subjective reason for accepting the warrant is that we have no knowledge of significant contradictory examples.

5 / Reasoning from Effect to Cause (sign reasoning)

This argument attempts to establish the existence of an event or condition. It takes one event as an indication of the presence of another event. The evidence for this argument is events, states, or conditions which are known to exist. The conclusion asserts the existence of the correlated event, usually a cause, so the argument moves from effect to cause or from effect to condition:

> When the Eisenhower administration recognized the Castro government in Cuba it admitted that it was in favor of that government, because recognition is a sign of approval in international politics.

The Eisenhower government recognized the Castro Cuban government. ⟶ The Eisenhower government approved of the Castro government.

When a government recognizes another government, this usually indicates that it approves of that government.

The warrant asserts a correlation between the type of event in the evidence and the type of event in the conclusion, so that when the first event occurs, it is likely that the second event can be asserted to have existed. The correlation may hold because the unobserved event is the direct cause of the data, as low air pressure causes a barometer to fall or troop movements may be directly caused by aggressive intentions. On the other hand, the causal relation may be indirect and the observed event may relate to a "condition" rather than a cause, e.g., free elections in a country may indicate a reasonably democratic government, since only democratic governments can permit free elections.

In evaluating argument from an effect to a cause, the strength of the correlation should be established. This requires testing of the principle stated in the warrant. The higher the correlation (the more frequent the association), the more certainly the effect can be taken as an indication of the cause. Secondly, other explanations for the evidence should be considered. The possibility should be considered that another event could have caused the data. If the relation is that of a "necessary" condition, the possibility of the event's existence without that condition should be evaluated.

6 / Reasoning from Circumstantial Evidence to a Hypothesis

This is closely related to argument from effect to cause. The process is one of explanation: The evidence presents facts and the conclusion presents a theory to account for the existence of those facts. In a murder trial, for example, the defendant may be charged with committing murder because his fingerprints, his hat, and his cigarette lighter were found at the scene of the crime and blood was found on his clothes. A hypothesis that he committed the murder would account for or explain all the data. This is the essence of the process: The conclusion, if true, must account for the data. The "accounting" is almost invariably a direct causal connection, the conclusion asserts an event which can causally produce the events of the data. The warrant asserts a relationship between the evidence and the conclusion.

Why has the Soviet Union not extended its power to the English Channel since the close of World War II? It is certainly not a lack of interest on the part of the rulers. Surely the one deterrent has been the overwhelming military power of the United States Strategic Air Command. If Russia tomorrow should move its troops toward the Atlantic Ocean, European territory would be conquered, but the Russian industrial centers would be destroyed from the air, and this would be a bad swap.

Russians have not ex-⟶ They have been deterred
tended their power over | by the Strategic Air Com-
Europe. | mand.

The fact that the Russians are afraid of retaliation by the Strategic Air Command would explain most completely (it is not through lack of interest) their inaction.

The difference between this and reasoning from sign should be observed. In reasoning from an effect to a cause there is a high correlation, *already known*, between the two types of events. The relation has occurred before with this specific type of event, and the strength of the argument depends upon the strength of the correlation. In reasoning from circumstantial evidence, the individual correlation between any one fact and the conclusion is low; only with other information or several facts does the conclusion gain probability. More than that, the hypothesis postulates new causal relations which could not have been correlated before in relation to the unique event described in the evidence. In the example we have used, we can assume that there is a cause for the inaction and that the cause is an inhibiting factor, but the specific condition which is the cause has not been correlated before with the events described by the data.

The distinction can be observed in analyzing a burglary. The evidence is that the local hardware store was burglarized. Footprints, a crowbar, a torn scrap of cloth, and blood stains on the broken door glass provide circumstantial evidence. The crowbar is traced to the purchaser. His footprints match and his hand has been recently cut. The cloth from the store matches a tear in a shirt he owns. Now if this person *did* burgle the store, that would account for the presence of his footprints, his cut hand, etc. Thus we have a new fact presented to explain a unique situation. It is a hypothesis. But suppose the police discover the door was opened in a particular way and the watchman was knocked unconscious. The case box lock has been picked, not broken. The police detect a method of operations which they have seen before and which they know is often used by Slithery Sam; a correlation between the pattern and Sam has been established. From the data the warrant allows the claim that Sam was present. The first event is a sign of the second.

The warrant asserts that the hypothesis is the most likely explanation (or cause) of the evidence. There are three important ways to establish this. The first is to show that the hypothesis satisfactorily explains the facts in the event in the simplest way possible. That is, if the hypothesis can explain the data with *one* fact, rather than several, then it is more likely. Secondly, its likelihood can be supported by eliminating other possible causes, showing that they did not exist or were not significant. Thirdly, if further information can be deduced from the hypothesis (if it is true it must have had other effects) and found to exist, then the probability of its truth increases.

In evaluating this process, certain questions are obvious: (1) Does the claim explain all the data? (2) Are enough facts given in the data to justify the hypothesis? (3) Are there any alternative hypotheses that are more likely? (4) Is there any contrary or contradictory information against the hypothesis? The last two are particularly important because the possibility of rival hypotheses will render the claim indeterminate until further investigation, and the advocate should carefully examine all possible information to formulate and modify his hypotheses. We remind you again not to let the hypothesis turn into an expectancy which sets you to interpret all data to confirm it. This leads to inaccurate claims, from paranoia and hypochrondria to belief in haunted houses. It is usually wise to have several tentative hypotheses in mind and investigate each one, using the methods we have described, before deciding upon a specific hypothesis.

7 / Reasoning from Cause to Effect

Reasoning from signs and from circumstantial evidence establishes past or present facts, reasoning from example establishes present patterns, but reasoning from cause leads to the claim of future facts. Because certain events exist, then certain other events are predicted: *A* is followed by *B*, and given *A*, this allows us to assert that *B* will exist:

> If the sanctions of the criminal law are removed, there is also removed one, if not the main, motive which at the present time influences homosexuals to consult medical advisors. The proportion of homosexuals who today consult medical advisors with regard to either their state or their behavior is admittedly small. Of those who do, a considerable proportion do so either because they have already found themselves in the hands of the police and have been sent in for examination, or because they desire expert evidence that may influence the court's outlook, or because circumstances have arisen that cause them to anticipate police attention. It appears, therefore, that even the small number who get medical examination will be reduced considerably if the laws against homosexuality are removed.

Legalization of homosexuality will remove pressures for homosexuals to seek medical care.	→	The number who seek medical care will be reduced.
When factors which influence people to do something are removed, then fewer persons will do that action.		

The evidence for this process is either events which exist or which are assumed to exist for the sake of the argument (as in the above). An example of an argument with evidence existing in the present would be: "Trade barriers have been eliminated in the European Common Market (evidence and cause), so we can predict an increase in the volume of trade among the member nations (conclusion and effect)." The second case occurs in predicting the consequences of possible policies or in considering the implications of possible events. The conclusion asserts that an event will occur in the future. It may be a general type of event, or it may be a specific event. The warrant is a causal generalization, which may be very complex. The warrant asserts that when events of type A occur, events of type B will follow. The generalization is not a simple one because events themselves are not simple. The effects of corruption in a union, the feasibility of certain plans for integration, the effects of a plan to control inflation, or almost any social issue where argumentative analysis may operate involves many factors, and their probability varies. As a result there is no precise formula by which one can calculate the likelihood of a war or the political effects of a policy. We can only make educated predictions.

In evaluating the argument, we must likewise make educated evaluations. If the events already exist, then the evidence must describe them enough to demonstrate that the factors contributing to the generalization in the warrant are present, that is, the event must come under the warrant. On the other hand, if the cause is a hypothetical proposal, the information must be based on projected plans, laws, blueprints, or given assumptions. Our study of rhetorical reasoning indicates that this prediction process is used most often in this hypothetical form, where it is used to consider consequences in propositions of action.

The warrant needs careful analysis. It may describe a variety of subjects at almost any level, e.g., appeasement leads to more demands; competition produces cheaper goods; dominating mothers cause their children to become neurotic; reinforcement causes the probability of the reinforced response to increase; higher pay for teachers will attract more persons into the field; trade barriers reduce trade. These warrants may be supported directly by examples, instances, or experiences, or they may be supported by a line of causal arguments, each of which can be evaluated. The strength of the argument depends upon the warrant, so let us consider the two types of support for a warrant in an argument which claims that government ownership of the railroads would result in inefficient management of them. The warrant would be a statement that most businesses that are owned by the government are inefficiently managed or that government ownership of businesses results in inefficient management. This generalization can be directly supported by citing examples of businesses owned by the government that are inefficiently managed or that became so after the government began to operate them. The generalization can also be supported through its component causal relations by showing the factors which would causally contribute to inefficiency: lack of competition, more red tape, bureaucracy, financial security, etc. These, in turn, are supported by examples. It is of utmost importance that the causal factors contributing to the relation are actually present in the evidence, which is to say that the examples used for backing must have common causal elements with the data.

In summary of the factors to evaluate in this argument:

(1) Is the causal warrant probable on the basis of its component relations? (2) Do examples confirm the warrant? (3) Does the data satisfy the warrant? (4) Are any factors present which would interfere with the effect, that is, are there any reservations present which would modify the relationship?

8 / Reasoning from a Comparison

In reasoning from comparison, one event is shown to be similar to another, and conclusions or statements about the first event are applied to the second. For example, because the city manager form of government worked well in River City, it will work well in Lakeburg, or because legalization of narcotics successfully controls addiction in England it would do the same here. The warrant is that if the situations are similar in their characteristics and relationships, then an assertion, conclusion, or description of one event can be made similarly about the other.

> In opposing this plan for a Federal program of college scholarships, I would point out that scholarships from private sources will stop if the program is inaugurated. In 1957 a government bill was considered which would have granted scholarships to forty students from each state. When the bill was announced, several corporations dropped their own plans for scholarship grants, and these were not resumed until the bill failed to pass Congress. The same thing will happen on a larger scale if these Federal scholarships are available on a national level.

When X bill was considered, several corporations dropped their plans for scholarships; and this bill is similar to X bill. ⟶ If this bill is passed, the same thing will happen; corporations will drop scholarship programs (and perhaps other sources will too).

If the bills are similar, their effect on private giving will be the same.

The comparison is a useful process of argument because it can be used to support many conclusions. It may be used to support a prediction or infer effects, as the example above illustrates. It may be used to justify a classification, e.g., an organization may be classed as "subversive" because of its similarities to an organization already classified as subversive. The lawyer uses this process when he cites precedent. He shows how the immediate case is similar to others previously adjudicated and concludes that the opinion in the previous cases should hold in the present case. Often he may point out the similarities but then extend or modify his conclusions on the basis of the unique features of the case in question.

The process is this: Two similar situations or events are presented. Event A is the situation about which the advocate wishes to draw a conclusion; event B is a factual situation of the same kind as the first situation. A statement which is true about event B is asserted to apply to event A. The two events and their similarities and the statement about event B make up the evidence. The statement applied to event A is the conclusion. The warrant is that the same relationships, facts, correlations, or characteristics apply in each situation and what may be said about one situation can also be said about the second situation.

The similarities between events A and B must be relevant to the conclusion to be drawn, or stated conversely, the conclusion must be related to the resemblances between the situations. Usually this means there is a causal relation among the demonstrated and the asserted similarities. If the underlying relationship is causal, then enough causal resemblances must be presented to indicate that a similar pattern or effect will be produced in event A. If, on the other hand, the resemblances are relevant to a classification or legal question (as in the "subversive" conclusion or a legal plea), the similarities demonstrated must be the ones we respond to in drawing the conclusion. That is, if we have classified an organization as subversive because it has

Nazi characteristics, such as belief in racial supremacy, advocacy of violence, etc., then to prove by comparison that a second organization is subversive, the characteristics which satisfy the criteria for "subversive" are the ones which should be compared. Whether the similarities for a particular argument are factual characteristics, structural relationships, or causal factors, the reasoning process is the same.

In evaluating reasoning from comparison, the first question is whether or not the resemblances are actually similar. If they are not, then no sound comparison is possible. Second, are the resemblances the essential or significant elements relative to the conclusion? The characteristics which are compared must be the causal determinants or be correlated with the characteristics in the conclusion, or they must be the defining characteristics. Further, an adequate number of elements must be compared for the inference to hold in the second situation. Finally, any dissimilarities in the two situations must be accounted for. If there are essential elements which are not similar, then the conclusion is less likely to hold. These dissimilarities may be discounted in three ways: (1) The advocate can assert that the differences are not essential or relevant to the conclusion. (2) He can modify the conclusion in the light of the differences. (3) He can modify a hypothetical position to adjust to the differences. To illustrate the first and third methods, let us look at the argument which states that because Britain legalizes the use of narcotics and is enabled to control narcotic addiction and drug traffic, the U. S. could do the same. A difference which might be presented is that Britain is a small country with a carefully regulated medical system. This could affect the effectiveness of the program. The advocate could defend his comparison (1) by demonstrating that the method of administration is not essential; it is the availability of narcotics which is the major element in control of addiction and traffic; or (2) he could propose a method of regulating and dispensing the drugs which will assure what control he deems necessary.

9 / *Reasoning from Figurative Analogy*

A brief comment needs to be made about the figurative analogy, which is weak as a form of argument, but nevertheless persuasive. The figurative analogy is not a comparison of factual elements (as is the comparison) but of abstract relationships or principles. The advocate wishes to draw a conclusion about situation A so he presents an analogous situation B as a method of providing insight or understanding. The analogy is more illustrative than probative, but as rhetoricians know, clear understanding may be most persuasive.

> Congressman X should not label everyone who is a liberal a Communist. After all, if you are spraying your roses against aphids, you do not use a spray which will kill all the animals and insects in the garden. Some of them are necessary and useful.

You would not attack aphids wisely if you used a spray which killed all insects; and calling all liberals Communists is like confusing all insects with aphids. ⟶ Calling all liberals Communists is not wise.

If your intent is to eliminate the cause of the problem, you should not eliminate elements that are not the cause.

In this analogy there is no attempt to assert that factual characteristics are alike. Rather, the general relations of intention and motive are similar. The analogy throws the primary situation (A) into another context in which the relationships can be seen more clearly. This may have the effect of clarifying the desires, intentions, and goals of the primary situation. The strength of the analogy—its quality of abstraction—is also its weakness. Any situation is so complex that many abstractions can be made from it, and analogies can often be reversed by extending them or presenting alternative conclusions. For example, an attack on the above analogy might point out that "if the roses are to be saved at all it might be necessary to use any and every means at hand, even if it means eliminating some harmless bugs."

To be of logical strength, the two situations compared must have similar relationships and these must be reasonable abstractions from the situations. That is, the factual characteristics of the primary situation must fall into the same relationships as the analogous situation. In using this process, the advocate should try to avoid analogies which can be reversed too obviously or too easily, and he should use analogies more for illustration than proof, for light rather than heat.

10 / Other Processes of Reasoning

The most important modes of reasoning have been described, but there are many others which are used in argumentation and advocacy. When an argument is encountered that does not fit into the patterns described, its conclusion and evidence should be explicitly phrased. Then a warrant should be formulated which will link the evidence and the conclusion. Remember that the warrant is a general principle which deals with types of events—the types of events described in the evidence and conclusion. It will sometimes help to formulate the warrant in an "if/then" form: "If a country buys grain on the world market, then its own crop has failed." Warrants may not always fit into this pattern, but in whatever way they are phrased they state a relationship between the evidence and the conclusion. Once the warrant is discovered it should be evaluated to determine its reliability. In poor arguments the relation in the warrant will be tenuous or even non-existent; in strong arguments the relation will be highly probable. Next the evidence and conclusion should be considered in relation to the warrant to determine if the entire unit is consistent. Finally, the evidence should be examined to discover if it does adequately fulfill the warrant.

USING REASONING PROCESSES

An understanding of these reasoning processes is important in inferring from evidence, in evaluating arguments, and in supporting conclusions. The first occurs most often in the investigation of a problem or proposition, when the investigator examines information to discover what conclusions may be drawn from it. He will soon arrive at hints of conclusions from the evidence in his research. He will also have a general idea of the kinds of conclusions which are relevant to his analysis. Chapter three describes "things to discover" about problems and propositions, and it should be reread to relate analysis to reasoning processes. The investigator should follow these hints of conclusions by doing further research into the types of evidence relevant to their proof. He should not try to prove or disprove conclusions, but he should discover as much evidence as possible and then infer the conclusions from that evidence. He should, however, let the principles of analysis and trends of evidence suggest what conclusions are relevant to his investigation.

In testing arguments the first step is to isolate the argument from the surrounding discourse and to explicitly formulate the evidence, warrant, and conclusion. As we have indicated, one of the elements is often assumed or not directly stated, in which case it must be inferred from the remaining two. Once the entire argument is made explicit it may be identified as one of the types described in this chapter, in which case it should be evaluated according to the particular requirements of that type of reasoning. If it is not a process explained here, then the advocate must determine what process it involves and what its requirements of proof are. This was discussed under the heading "other processes of reasoning." Particular attention should be paid to the warrant, since it establishes the relation between evidence and conclusion as a general principle. This process of evaluation will be described in more detail in the next chapter.

In developing proof through reasoning the advocate should move through the two steps just discussed, i.e., his own conclusions should be based on the evidence which he has discovered, and his reasoning processes should be carefully evaluated. In proof he will usually support his conclusions with the evidence resulting from his research, the very evidence which has led him to those very conclusions. However, he can strengthen his proof by devoting research to discover additional evidence of high quality. A second way of strengthening conclusions is to develop other reasoning processes which will support them. To do this the advocate should examine his conclusion carefully and consider what other types of argument will lead to it. For example, a conclusion asserting that country X is arming for aggression can be supported initially by argument from effect to cause, sign reasoning. It can also be supported by reasoning from cause to effect and reasoning from comparison. In this way the advocate should consider several different processes of reasoning which might lead to the conclusion. These processes will suggest kinds of evidence to seek out, and if the evidence confirms the conclusion, it can be used as additional proof. This latter procedure can be used for the advocate in discovering arguments to support a given conclusion. That is, he can examine the conclusion and determine what kind of proof processes will support it, then search for the evidence necessary for such proof.

►NOTES◄

1. This description of the elements of an argument is based on one devised by Stephen Toulmin, in *The Uses of Argument* (New York: Cambridge University Press, 1958). A more detailed application of the pattern to argument is found in Chapter eight of *Decision by Debate*, by Douglas Ehninger and Wayne Brockriede (New York: Dodd, Mead & Company, Inc., 1963), pp. 98-109.

2. Another discussion by Mr. Hastings of these modes of reasoning will be found in *Reason in Controversy*, by Glen Mills (Boston: Allyn and Bacon, 1964). For a more detailed analysis of the processes involved, see "A Reformulation of the Modes of Reasoning in Argumentation," pp. 22-147, by Arthur Hastings, an unpublished Ph.D. dissertation at Northwestern University. However, the formulation presented in this chapter modifies in some ways both of the above references.

3. Descriptions of value systems other than ours clearly illustrate the role of value judgments in social issues. It is instructive for the advocate to study other cultural value systems and attempt to formulate arguments leading to value judgments based on those systems. These references are recommended as introductions to other value structures: *Patterns of Culture,* by Ruth Benedict (New York: Mentor Books, 1958). *Freedom and Culture,* by Dorothy Lee (Englewood Cliffs, N. J.: Spectrum Books, 1959), especially the essays "Are Basic Needs Ultimate?," pp. 70-77, "Symbolization and Value," pp. 78-88, and "Linguistic Reflection of Wintu Thought," pp. 121-130.

4. A sound and pleasant discussion of statistical evidence and its faults is found in *How to Lie with Statistics,* by Darrell Huff (New York: W. W. Norton & Company, Inc., 1954). This enlightening book should be read by all advocates.

5. That is, for any specific example there is the assertion of a causal relation, e.g., Anthony robbed the store

because he read about a robbery in a comic book; Smith is doing better work because you complimented him. To prove that factor A is the cause of factor B usually requires comparing the factors present with known causal relations and the elimination of other possible causes. For a logician's approach to causal analysis see Chapter twelve on causal connections in the second edition of *Introduction to Logic*, by Irving Copi (New York: The Macmillan Company, 1960), pp. 355-415.

► E X E R C I S E S ◄

1. Construct an argument to illustrate each of the types of reasoning described in this chapter. Use actual evidence and acceptable warrants to support your conclusions.

2. Examine one of the following specimens of advocacy. Identify each argument used by the advocate and separate it into evidence, warrant, and conclusion. Remember, some elements may not be stated explicitly. Classify each argument according to the processes described in this chapter or, if it is not described here, discover what the underlying process is. Write a paragraph evaluating the evidence, warrant, and conclusion for each argument.

   a. Edmund Burke, "Conciliation with America," in Chauncey Goodrich, *Select British Eloquence* (Indianapolis: The Bobbs-Merrill Company, 1963), pp. 266-291.

   b. Thomas Waring, "The South's Case for Desegregation," in William Petersen and David Matza (eds.), *Social Controversy* (Belmont, Calif.: Wadsworth, 1963), pp. 175-183.

   c. Douglas MacArthur, "Address to Congress," in Carroll Arnold, Douglas Ehninger, and John Gerber (eds.), *The Speaker's Resource Book* (Chicago: Scott, Foresman and Company, 1961), pp. 275-280.

d. Clarence Darrow, "Crime and Criminals," in Arnold, Ehninger, and Gerber, *The Speaker's Resource Book,* pp. 137-142.

e. Either of the opening speeches by John Kennedy and Richard Nixon in the first television debate of the 1960 Presidential campaign, in Sidney Kraus (ed.), *The Great Debates* (Bloomington, Ind.: Indiana University Press, 1962), 348 ff.

f. A first affirmative constructive speech from any debate in Russel Windes and Arthur Kruger, *Championship Debating* (Portland, Me.: J. Weston Walch, 1961).

3. Prepare and present a five-minute speech in which at least two processes of reasoning are used to support conclusions.

4. Write a two- to three-page essay of advocacy in which at least two types of reasoning are used to support conclusions.

CRITICAL REFUTATION

We turn now to the refutation of arguments. The previous chapters have focused on investigating and proving a proposition or a conclusion. But often the advocate will speak or write against the acceptance of a proposition. The lawyer may contend that Smith did not defame Jones' character; opponents of Federal aid to secondary schools may deny there is a serious shortage of school teachers and facilities; proponents of civil rights may attack assertions that there are racial differences in intellectual ability. No matter what the position of the advocate, whether he speaks for a proposition or against one, he will need knowledge of ways to attack arguments. If he speaks for a proposition, he must be prepared to refute opposing arguments or conclusions which the audience holds, as well as refute attacks on his arguments by opposing speakers or writers. If he speaks against a proposition, the advocate must refute arguments which support the proposition.

THE SCENES OF REFUTATION

Since a controversy by its definition must have more than one possible conclusion, at least to someone, an advocate must be prepared to face various arguments opposing his position. Books may be written to answer arguments in previous books, or an article may be published by a magazine in one issue and an answering article in the next issue. Letters to the editor may take up cudgels against or for a contributor's conclusions. Some publications print simultaneous pro and con articles about an issue.

In the case of letters to the editor or successive articles, the writer who follows has the opportunity to know and study the arguments which are advanced for the opposing position. Often in the case of simultaneous publication each author will have the opportunity of seeing the opposing article before the final draft of his own paper. Perhaps most often an advocate will write a book or article in the contest of a controversy but without a specific essay or advocate in opposition. In all of these cases refutation is present, but its role varies. It may be directed against specific arguments presented by advocates. This is especially the case in successive articles or letters, for here the advocate has something to answer. On the other hand, when the writing is more generally addressed the writer still may wish to refute general arguments which his readers might believe. The advocate must anticipate what opposing arguments his audience might know or hold, and he should try to refute them in his own presentation.

In oral discourse, similar situations occur. The advocate may be speaking in "isolation," that is, as a single speaker supporting a proposition before an audience. In this case he must anticipate what opposing arguments may be present in the minds of the audience and attempt to refute them in his speech. If his speech is in the context of a current public issue, with speeches, editorializing, and general discussion, he can speak to specific arguments or conclusions which have been presented previously; here his refutation is directed. Finally, the speaker may be engaged in a debate, in which two or more speakers appear on the same platform to present their views on an issue of controversy between them. Thus did Abraham Lincoln and Stephen Douglas debate in 1858 over the questions of slavery, democracy, and federalism. And thus did Richard Nixon and John Kennedy debate in 1960 over the issues facing the holder of the Presidency. But debates are not limited to those of political ambitions. Witnesses presenting testimony before congressional committees may find themselves debating, in effect, with other witnesses who appear. Representatives at decision-making meetings, from city councils to legislatures, engage in debate when they argue differing positions on an issue. In these situations, refutation must be fast, penetrating, and judicious. The advocate must immediately respond to the important arguments in the most effective way.[1]

THE PROCESS OF REFUTATION

The advocate should remember that the purpose of refutation is always to cast doubt on or deny a conclusion. In terms of psychological effect, an attack on minor evidence may influence some attitudes, but it is the validity of the conclusion that the advocate and the audience should (and usually do!) consider most important. There are two principal ways to refute a conclusion. The first is by attacking its proof, demonstrating that the argument is unsound. The second approach is to overturn the conclusion by proving a contrary conclusion, that is, proving an opposite or inconsistent conclusion better and with more force. Where possible the careful advocate will deal with opposing arguments in both ways. He will demonstrate that the proof is deficient, then go further to prove a counter argument.

STRATEGY IN REFUTATION

The advocate begins to prepare his refutation in the stage of analysis we have labeled "counter-analysis," in which he studies the evidence and arguments which oppose his position. Abraham Lincoln was asked his secret of winning law cases. He replied that it was knowing the opposition case better than the opposing lawyer did. This certainly holds true for every advocate. He must investigate *all* of the problem's complexities, and he should make a point of considering even the arguments against the side which he considers the strongest (which is his side, we trust). He should analyze the requirements of proof for the opposition. He will thus know what must be done to prove the opposing position. Then he should investigate the opposing arguments to discover how well they can satisfy the requirements of proof, studying these arguments with the same thoroughness he devotes to his own position. In this way he will know what they establish and what they do not establish. He will know what evidence is against him and how it can be used. With such information he is prepared to discover and plan refutation to attack the opposing position and to defend his own arguments.

In the heat of battle, which arguments should be refuted? Usually the advocate cannot attack or answer all arguments advanced, simply because time or space will not permit it. He must be selective, and it is possible to set up a hierarchy to determine what refutation is of most significance. The most important attack which can be made is on the over-all analysis of the proposition. This is the attack that a *prima-facie* case has not been presented. This type of refutation should come first in attacking an affirmative position and it should be the first attack to be refuted in defending an affirmative position. For example, a speaker may advocate emphasis on college athletics at a particular school for the reasons that (1) alumni support is beneficial, (2) a national reputation is desirable, and (3) school spirit would help the institution. An attack on the analysis would be to contend that the relation between athletics and the three benefits has not been established. When some issues are omitted or essential causal links are not established, then this logical incompleteness is of first importance to attacker and defender.

Analysis resolves the proposition into issues, and after an attack on analysis, the next most important attack is one on the proof or the issues or the contentions. Indeed, it is usually on the issues that most of the attack and defense will focus. Obviously the affirmative advocate should have a clear understanding of what the issues of his case are so he can devote most of his time to establishing them. Identically, on the negative side, an understanding of the issues enables an affective attack on the affirmative support of the proposition. Chapter three and Chapter seven describe how propositions are analyzed into and proved through their issues, and advocates should know these methods of analysis and use them automatically to focus their attention on the issues.

Of next and sometimes equal psychological importance is any argument which has received sufficient attention to make it seem important. Even if the argument is minor in the total context, if it has received much emphasis in time or space then it should be dealt with immediately. The logical importance of arguments is often overshadowed by their psychological effect, and so the advocate must remember this in his analysis of the audience. The effect of such arguments does not mean that the advocate must always spend an equal amount of time on his part, for he may be able to dismiss such items with a few brief sentences, but they should receive his attention regardless.

The next argument type for refutation can be labeled the "argument for effect." Whatever the advocate can attack effectively and impressively, or whatever he can defend effectively and impressively, he should turn to. His initial consideration must go to attacks and defenses of vital logical and psychological arguments, but then he should give precedence to attacks and defenses which he can present with good effect on the audience. Of course, even a *prima-facie* case and the selection of issues will be done by the affirmative advocate with the audience in mind, so there will be some consideration of the psychological importance of the logical arguments, but we are referring to arguments which are not so logically important as the issues, and unless the advocate has time to present all the possible refutation, he should at least select the attacks or defenses which he can present most effectively.

ATTACKING THE PROOF

Refutation of an argument should be presented both to criticize the proof and to challenge for adequate proof. If the evidence is insufficient, let us say, in argument from example to generalization, the advocate should point out that one example is inadequate to lead to a generalization, perhaps also showing that the generalization is too complex to be based on just one example. Then he should go further to explain what must be done to establish the conclusion, that is, he could ask for several examples from varying contexts, each exhibiting the pattern generalized. Thus the advocate not only attacks the proof used in the argument, but he defines the *requirements of proof* which must be used for the argument. This serves two functions. First it causes the audience to look at the argument from your point of view. They will examine further argument with the requirements of proof in mind, they will be able to tell whether or not the conclusion has been established. Thus you may be able to forestall an audience accepting any reply to your objection just because it was made; now they are alerted to what must be presented if the reply is to be valid. Unfortunately, in a written or oral controversy the audience often responds to the *fact* of a reply rather than to the *content* of a reply. With this approach you try to make the audience more discriminating. The second function of describing the requirements of proof when you attack an argument is that it establishes the reasonableness of your own character. It does this by implicitly demonstrating that you are willing to be convinced on the basis of evidence and reasoning. It is persuasive to take this position, and it is also reasonable, since this should be the actual attitude of the ethical and wise advocate.

This process should be used at every level of proof. If the evidence is faulty, the type of evidence required should be described. If the warrant is not a reasonable one, the refutation should include an explanation of what evidence and principles (warrants) are required to establish the conclusion. (In referring to warrants, it is best to use the terms "assumptions" and "underlying principles," since audiences are not familiar with this term. "Evidence" and "conclusion" are commonly understood.) If the analysis of the proposition omits issues, the advocate can focus on the ignored arguments and show why each is important and must be proved by the opponent. In this manner, the advocate can influence the audience to evaluate the arguments and arrive at conclusions on rational processes, and if the advocate's own argument has such bases, his position is more likely to be accepted.

ATTACKING THE EVIDENCE

Chapter four describes many of the inadequacies which may be present in evidence *per se*. Poor information and evidence should be pointed out as such, for no proof can be strong if it rests on untrue, out of date, limited, or incomplete information. The advocate should automatically examine opposing proofs for the quality of the evidence, keeping in mind the characteristics of the evidence relative to the particular source and field of knowledge. In attacking evidence which is unsound the advocate should not just point out that it is, say, out of date or obscure. He should insist that a valid conclusion cannot be drawn from such evidence and he should explain the quality of evidence which is necessary, urging the audience to reject the argument until acceptable evidence is presented.

Evidence should next be viewed in relation to the rest of the elements of the argument. Each type of reasoning process requires certain kinds of evidence. In reasoning from example, the instances must be typical of their type. In reasoning from circumstantial evidence there must be a sufficient number of facts to justify the hypothesis. The conclusion of an argument is not proved unless the evidence is actually what the warrant requires. This is saying, in ordinary language, that the conclusion does not follow from the evidence, the information is not adequate, not the right kind, or otherwise does not lead to the conclusion. Chapter five has described what evidence each type of reasoning requires, and the advocate should habitually test the evidence to determine if it satisfies the warrant which will lead to the conclusion. To do this he may have to infer the warrant or warrants which lead to the conclusion. An example of this type of analysis has been given in Chapter five in the argument that there is misadministration in the system of unemployment compensation. And consider this argument:

> Senator Snort is against the cause of peace. We know this must be the case because he has continually criticized the Committee for a Sane Nuclear Policy, which is working for a peaceful world.

Here we have an argument from circumstantial evidence to a hypothesis, in which an attitude of the senator is hypothesized because it would explain his actions. However, a critical attack on the evidence would be that it does not provide enough factual information to support the hypothesis, and more evidence is needed before the conclusion can be considered probable.

ATTACKING THE WARRANT

The conclusion may fail also because the warrant is faulty. Since the warrant is a general principle which states a link between the evidence and the conclusion, that principle or relation must be true or highly probable for the conclusion to follow. There are two ways to challenge warrants. One is to show that the relation expressed in the warrant is not likely or not true. First the warrant must be identified. This is done by stating the evidence and the conclusion and formulating a general principle which will connect the two elements. To illustrate this, let us use this argument:

> Mr. Kennedy came to office on the vote of less than a majority of the electorate. Thus, from the start, he could not hope to command the support of half of the citizens who vote.

| Kennedy received less than a majority from the electorate. | ⟶ | Kennedy could not command the support of a majority of the electorate from the start. |

A general principle must now be found relating the types of events described in the two elements. The warrant must be something like, "If a candidate cannot get votes from some persons, neither can he command their support if he is elected." Once this assumption in the argument is discovered, it can be attacked as not true. The same procedure can be followed for any argument; the conclusion and evidence are identified, a warrant is formulated to link the two, and finally the warrant is examined to test its probability. To present this type of attack to the ordinary audience you may refer to the warrant as an assumption. "My opponent is making this assumption in his argument," you say, stating the assumption and showing that it is false. "Is it true that if you did not vote for a person you will not support him if he is elected? No. One of the reasons for the success of democracy is that we *do* support the elected officials." Sometimes the stating of the assumption will be sufficient to show that it is false, but it may be necessary to demonstrate its weaknesses. "Lincoln, Wilson, and Truman were all minority presidents, and yet once they were elected they were supported, even though there were disagreements on their policies."

Some warrants may be open to a more involved attack. Reservations or qualifications may be made on their accuracy or range. Since rhetorical arguments are all based on probabilities, the warrants which deal with matters of fact are only probable, not certain. An examination of the warrants for the arguments cited in this book will reveal that they are almost all probable, not certain. There are always reservations to their application—the examples may not be typical, there may be other definitions, alternative hypotheses are possible. Such warrants can be attacked on this basis, the advocate demonstrating that it has too many reservations for it to be applied without further evidence.

> Lascivia is buying wheat on the world grain market. Therefore their domestic wheat crop must be a failure.

Lascivia is buying wheat ⎯⎯⎯⎯→ Lascivia's domestic wheat on the world grain market.　　　　crop must be a failure.

The argument is from effect to cause, and the warrant would be "When a country buys wheat on the world market, this indicates that its own crop is a failure." This warrant has a degree of probability, and we know it has often been the case. However, it is not a principle which is always true, and there are several other possible causes of buying wheat, e.g., the desire to stockpile, increased domestic demand, correction of a trade balance, etc. Thus the warrant can be amended to read, "When a country buys wheat on the world market, this indicates its own crop is a failure, unless its domestic demand has increased, unless it is stockpiling wheat, etc." In presenting this refutation the advocate would identify the assumption inherent in the argument and then explain the reservations or exceptions to it. He should use the method we have previously described, that of stating what must be established for the warrant to be valid. In this example the advocate would insist that the alternative possibilities be eliminated with evidence to show they are not the case. Each type of reasoning process has a particular kind of warrant and each warrant can be attacked in the context of its argument in specific ways. We will summarize briefly ways in which each reasoning process may be attacked in this way, with the reminder that we are describing what we feel is generally the most useful method, though there are others.

Reasoning from Characteristics to a Description. The warrant comprises criteria of definition, which may be challenged by claiming that additional or different criteria are necessary. That the definition is incorrect may be shown by presenting examples which contain similar characteristics but which would not be described in the same way. For example, suppose a warrant defines "invasion" as an "unprovoked attack by one country on another." This definition can be challenged by pointing out that the guerrilla attacks in Southeast Asia are not considered invasion, nor is the shooting down of a reconnaissance plane.

Reasoning from Characteristics to a Value Judgment. The values asserted by the warrants can be directly challenged. This may be done by attacking the value system in which they are rooted or by confrontation with contrary or alternative values. Consider the warrant which states, "Instability in marriage is bad for the community." This may be directly challenged: "What is so bad about instability? There are many aspects of community life which are not static, and they do not seem to harm the community." Or contrary values may be adduced: "It is better for persons unhappily married to be divorced than to have a marriage of hate and unhappiness—if that is instability it is nevertheless good." Warrants may also be attacked for not including sufficient criteria to make a value judgment, as if the merit of a newspaper, political policy, or racehorse could be judged on one or two qualities alone.

Reasoning from Example to a Descriptive or Causal Generalization. Since the warrant asserts that the examples are representative, the most effective refutation for this type of argument is to present examples which are contrary to the generalization.

Reasoning from Effect to Cause. The warrant usually asserts that the conclusion is the cause of the evidence, and the most effective attack is to present other possible causes. An example of this approach is the above argument on the purchase of wheat. There it was pointed out that there could be other causes which would produce the same event. Sometimes the warrant is a correlation in which one event is known to be associated with another. The warrant asserts, "We have found that when event A exists, event B also exists." An assertion of causality is not made. The best attack on this warrant is to present examples in which one event occurred without the other, thus casting doubt on the reliability of the connection. An example of this is the argument earlier in this chapter (see pp. 198-99) on the relation between voting and support for a political candidate.

Reasoning from Circumstantial Evidence to a Hypothesis. The warrant in this process asserts that the conclusion best explains the evidence. An attack on this is to present alternative hypotheses which could equally well or better account for the evidence, e.g., Perry Mason discovers that it was not his client but another person who committed the crime. The advocate may simply present alternative hypotheses with the suggestion that the conclusion is uncertain until they are eliminated, or he may wish to propose an alternate hypothesis, as does Mason, warranting that it better accounts for the evidence.

Reasoning from Cause to Effect. The warrant is the assertion of a causal connection between events: A's are followed by B's, or A's cause B's. But causal relations in social issues are complex and such warrants have many reservations and exceptions. These may be factors which will nullify the cause, intervene between the cause and the effect, or counteract the effect.

> This bill will raise teachers' salaries in our state; therefore, we will have more college graduates go into teaching here.

The warrant asserts that higher salaries in teaching will cause more college graduates to go into the field. The three methods of attack could be (1) the cost of living will rise enough to counteract the increase; (2) because more teachers are required, the money will not go as far, and over-all salaries will not increase; (3) graduates will not go into teaching because it is a low-status profession.

Reasoning from Comparison. The warrant asserts that the conclusion follows because of essential similarities. The attack on this is to present dissimilarities which are essential to the conclusion.

Reasoning from Figurative Analogy. The most effective attack on the warrants of analogies is to carry them out until they become absurd or ridiculous. Usually in the situations compared there are elements which can support alternate conclusions, and the advocate can use them to reverse the analogy and turn the tables on the original conclusion. This is illustrated on pp. 183-84.

Summary of methods of attacking the proof:[2]

Evidence:

1. Is it true, accurate, complete, *per se?* Does it say what it presumes to say?
2. Is it complete, adequate, and satisfactory in regard to what is required by the warrant and the conclusion?

Warrant:

1. If a warrant is given, does it lead from the evidence to the conclusion?
2. Is the necessary warrant true to a high degree of probability?

3. Are there qualifications, exceptions, or reservations to the warrant?

Conclusion:

1. Can acceptable evidence be combined with a reliable warrant to lead to this conclusion?

OVERTURNING THE CONCLUSION WITH COUNTER PROOF

The second approach to refutation is to prove an opposite or inconsistent conclusion. Evidence and a warrant are presented which will lead to a conclusion opposing the argument under attack. For example, a proponent of segregation might argue that cultural differences between Southern whites and Negroes require segregated schools. In refutation of this an advocate might contend that the differences actually present a need for integrated schools, which will remove those differences.

This approach is logically possible with any of the processes of reasoning which we have described in the previous chapter. In reasoning from characteristics to a description or a value judgment, a contrary conclusion can be established by presenting additional characteristics or interpreting the characteristics in a different way. In the *Rhetoric* Aristotle illustrates how people can be described in different ways through different labeling of the same characteristics. Similar behavior may be classified as brave or foolhardy, an indifferent man may be reclassified as easygoing, or a thrifty person described as a miser. In reasoning from examples to generalizations, a sufficient number or quality of contrary examples can not only disprove the generalization, but also create some probability for another conclusion. Causal arguments are often amenable to attack by this method, because social controversies are complex and many causal elements or relations are present. Our discussion of causal processes of reasoning indicates that other causal factors may invalidate conclusions and lead to other claims. Here particularly the research and analysis of the advocate is important, since this will give him an understanding of the factual relationships involved. It would seem that arguments using comparisons cannot so often be attacked in this way because they will rarely be used if they could lead to inconsistent conclusions. Analogies, however, may often be turned around, as we have illustrated in our discussion of them. Further, it is most easy to find another analogy to support the opposite conclusion.

In overturning conclusions the advocate may use the same mode of reasoning which was used to establish the opposing argument. However, other methods of reasoning should be used as well. An argument established by cause-to-effect reasoning may be attacked by using a comparison or an argument from sign. Whatever arguments the advocate uses for refutation he should make them as strong as possible, with adequate evidence, acceptable warrants, and hence logical conclusions. Otherwise his counter-arguments would be subject to attack and would avail little.

Briefly, in refutation the advocate should first analyze the opposing argument to discover weaknesses in its proof. He should attack those weaknesses, selecting the most significant faults for primary attention. Finally he should show the conclusion is false by establishing a contrary argument with satisfactory evidence and warrant. Not always will the advocate use all of these approaches or all of the methods of attack, but he should consider all the possible methods of refutation and select the most effective for use against the argument.

PRESENTATION OF REFUTATION

For refutation to be effective it must be presented clearly and relevantly, whether written or oral. The advocate's audience should know exactly what the attack is and how it affects the opposing argument. We suggest a three-step presentation for this purpose:

1. Statement of the argument to be refuted
2. Refutation: attack of the proof or overturning of the conclusion
3. A statement that the argument has been refuted, showing how it affects the over-all position of the opposition

Inasmuch as the advocate will rarely wish to attack every possible fault in proof, he must make clear exactly what he *is* attacking. By stating the opposing argument at the beginning of his refutation, he will direct the attention of the audience to that particular unit of proof. Then the advocate should describe the proof that was used and explain its weakness, making clear what is required for an adequate argument for the conclusion. He may, if possible, support an alternative conclusion through evidence and warrant, or this may be done *instead of* the attack on the original proof. Finally the advocate should summarize the destruction of the conclusion and show how this affects the total argument of the opposing position.

►NOTES◄

1 For reference to written and spoken debates, see the exercises at the end of Chapters six and seven.
2. A discussion of fallacious reasoning will be found in W. Ward Fearnside and William B. Holther, *Fallacy: The Counterfeit of Argument* (Englewood Cliffs, N. J.: Prentice-Hall, Inc., 1959). The book contains a wealth of poor arguments (intentionally, that is) which will give the advocate practice in detecting and analyzing weaknesses in reasoning.

►EXERCISES◄

1. Write a one-paragraph refutation for each of the arguments used in Chapter five as illustrations for each of

the modes of reasoning (the diagrammed examples). Concentrate on attacking the proof rather than overturning the conclusion with other proof.

2. Write a two- to three-page letter to the editor refuting one of the essays from William Petersen and David Matza (eds.), *Social Controversy* (Belmont, Calif.: Wadsworth, 1963), or refuting an article in a recent issue of *Harper's Magazine, Atlantic Monthly, The Reporter,* or *National Review*.

3. Present a five-minute speech refuting an essay described in Exercise 2.

4. Write a three- to four-page paper describing the refutation methods used in one of the following.

   a. Abraham Lincoln, "Cooper Union Address," in many collections of speeches, including W. M. Parrish and Marie Hochmuth (eds.), *American Speeches* (New York: Longmans, Green, & Co., Inc., 1954), pp. 285-304.

   b. The first Nixon-Kennedy debate in the 1960 Presidential campaign, in Sidney Kraus (ed.), *The Great Debates* (Bloomington, Ind.: Indiana University Press, 1962), pp. 348-368.

   c. Any debate from Russel Windes and Arthur Kruger, *Championship Debating* (Portland, Me.: J. Weston Walch, 1961).

   d. Any of the other debates listed in Exercise 2 for Chapter seven.

▶ 7 ◀ PERSUASIVE PROOF: CONSTRUCTING A CONVINCING CASE

In argumentation there are two concepts of proof. One is proof in relation to the most objective logical requirements and the other is proof in terms of what will convince a particular audience. In this chapter we will define "proof" as "that which causes an audience to believe or accept a conclusion as true on the basis of the evidence and reasoning presented by the advocate."[1] This chapter will answer two questions: How does the advocate make his evidence, reasoning, and hence conclusions convincing to his audience; and how does he construct cases to support the proposition from that evidence and reasoning?

PERSUASIVE ARGUMENT

The basic principle of proof is that the arguments the advocate uses should be linked to beliefs, attitudes, values, and facts which the audience will accept. All proof must ultimately be grounded in statements which the audience believes. The audience must believe the evidence if they are to believe the conclusion. And the warrants used, because they are general principles which lead to the conclusions, must also be accepted by the audience, even though the warrants may not be explicit in the statement of the argument.[2]

But what if the audience will not accept part of the argument used by the advocate to establish his conclusion? In this event, which is not unusual, the advocate must establish the elements of his argument with preliminary arguments which *do* begin with elements acceptable to the audience, and which lead to his final argument. This does not necessarily mean that the advocate must catalog the facts and generalizations which the audience already has verbalized and believes or that he must then figure out some way to build from them his final proposition. This might be rather difficult. In the first place, most warrants which the advocate will use are general principles which will be accepted by the audience or will require only a once-removed argument. And even though the audience may not have the specific information about the subject— the statistics, circumstances, characteristics, etc.—it may very well accept the information on the authority of the advocate. That is, one of its attitudes is an attitude toward the advocate, and this will usually be one of trust unless his assertions seem unreasonable or there are outside reasons to doubt him.

The advocate should never present an argument which he knows to be untrue or improbable, and he should remain true to the requirements of proof of his proposition. If we are to recommend argumentation and advocacy as the best means for public and private decision-making, then the processes should not be distorted either in our own investigation or in our public advocacy. The elements and processes of proof must receive their just emphasis—no more and no less than their relative importance. There are important advantages to this ethical position. First, the advocate's position is protected against some refutation if the audience knows the complete reasoning process which establishes his proposition. Second, the advocate and the audience will both have a reasonable and realistic understanding of the proof and are more likely to believe in it firmly. Third, a pattern of response is set up in which the audience expects to evaluate arguments rationally, which is to the advantage of the advocate and society.

This should not be taken to imply that the advocate must deliver detailed, dull speeches, and write tracts of trivia. Because an argument is logical does not mean it is dull. It may be logical, exciting, stimulating, moving, and forceful at the same time. The emotional response to an argument depends on the audience's personal involvement with the subject matter, and the advocate should always try to make his arguments meaningful and personal to his audience. What we are saying is that an argument should be both emotional and reasonable, but it should not be exciting without evidence, inciting without warrant. These latter practices are unethical and destroy the values which argumentation embodies.

Our position also does not imply that the advocate must always present his entire case, or even a *prima-facie* case each time he speaks or writes. What he presents to an audience is determined by his purpose and the response he seeks. He may prefer to outline his arguments for the proposition without proving them specifically, as a political candidate might present his platform before a general audience. On the other hand, the advocate may go into the entire proof of his case, as an economist might do before a specialized congressional committee. Often the advocate will find it wisest to deal with one small aspect of the total proposition in order to open his audience's mind or modify their attitudes, waiting until other times, other places to complete his case. But he must remain faithful to the standards of logical proof and claim only what he purports to prove. He should not claim to have established his proposition when he has, in fact, proved only a portion of the arguments relating to it.

Our emphasis on adapting to the audience and basing arguments on their beliefs must not be misinterpreted. We are not taking the position that the advocate must prove what the audience wants to believe. He cannot be responsible to the requirements of proof of the proposition if he subordinates his argument to the preferences of the audience. Our view on audience analysis is that the advocate must discover and utilize beliefs of the audience which will lead to his arguments if those arguments are to be convincing.

ANALYZING THE ADVOCATE'S AUDIENCE

1 / *What Occasions the Audience?*

There are ways of analyzing an audience which will be helpful to the advocate in planning his proof. The first is a careful description of the circumstances under which they become an audience for advocacy and the implications which can be drawn from those occasions. These occasions may be either for written or spoken material.

Written Advocacy. In this medium the advocate should consider how the audience will obtain his writing. If the argument is in book form for commercial sales, purchasers will buy the book only if they are interested in the subject. Their reading, in general, will be a reflection of interest which is already present. If the book is to be directed toward a particular area, e.g., politics, science, etc., the author can assume that the readers have some knowledge of the subject. He may, of course, choose to direct the writing to any level of knowledge on the part of those who read the book. If the material is to appear in a magazine, the educational level of the readers and the general tenor of the periodical will be important. However, general magazines from *Reader's Digest* to *Harper's* are read cover to cover rather than selectively, so the advocate cannot be guaranteed of the level of interest or knowledge associated with selective choice. Other written advocacy may appear in pamphlets, tracts, or letters. Certainly the advocate will realize that persons already concerned with the controversy, pro or con, will read such material. But it will also be presented to many who have no interest in or awareness of the problem, and he should consider these persons part of his audience and construct his proof with them in mind.

Spoken Advocacy. In the analysis of audiences listening to advocacy, both the occasion and the audience's size must be considered. For certain occasions the speaker will have the interest, if not the total agreement, of the audience. Open lectures, political rallies, and meetings called for special purposes are all occasions in which most people in the audience attend because they are already interested or want to be interested. In addition, at political rallies, sales meetings, and similar purposeful gatherings, the audience is usually in agreement about the purpose of the meeting. By analyzing the occasion, the advocate can discover what beliefs or attitudes the audience holds toward the elements of his arguments. The size of the audience is relevant to the response to his arguments. In a small group, perhaps up to fifty persons, there is more interaction, less social or mass response, and more informality in behavior than in a larger audience. This size of audience can probably be directed more easily to detailed consideration of complex arguments than can a larger audience, which has more drains on its attention and seems to require more simple presentations. For this small group audience the advocate can probably go into more detail in his proof and can probably be assured of more thoughtful attention than with a larger audience, though if a person is an effective speaker, the differences in audience size may not be significant. With a larger audience, the size one would find in anything from a small auditorium to a large arena, the factor of social facilitation begins to occur. This means that as one member of the audience responds in a particular way, he stimulates other members around him to respond in the same way, and a "chain reaction" may result. It is partly this process which turns audiences into mobs, produces riots, and encourages gang wars. On the other hand, and for the same reason, large audiences tend to be more formal on formal occasions. As we mentioned before, they are more easily distracted from the speaker because of distance and the environment. They also tend to be more personally isolated from individual neighbors than in a more intimate group, despite the social facilitation. As a result of these factors the large audience may be more responsive to simpler arguments than complex ones unless measures are taken to counter these variables, such as the use of humor to create empathy, the emphasis on arguments which motivate, and the creation of personal involvement on the part of the audience.

The audience for a television or radio speech is usually composed of one or two persons around the set. These persons are listening by choice and can leave the speaker by turning a dial. Their choice will be determined by their initial interest in the subject and by the interest which the advocate generates. They have the opportunity at all times of withdrawing attention, either deliberately or unconsciously. Evidence indicates that most people listen to radio speeches with preconceptions, and then tend to listen to arguments with which they are in agreement or about which they are curious. Much of the effect of the speech on these people depends on their preconceptions. For example, Republicans who listened to the Nixon-Kennedy debates in 1960 tended to listen with close attention to Nixon and with little attention to Kennedy and then conclude that Nixon had won. The opposite tendency was true of the Democratic listeners.[3] The advocate should consider this problem in developing his arguments for broadcast presentation. He may wish to include material to motivate persons of opposing sentiments to listen, and he may want to make his evidence and warrants unusually clear for those who are not committed.

2 / *What Are the Beliefs of the Audience?*

The advocate must know what the beliefs of the audience are that will relate to his case. These questions will indicate some of the relevant types of information the advocate should try to discover.

A. *What are their values and attitudes?* Almost every proposition requires some reference to a value system, and the advocate should support his position with values the audience holds or he should directly establish the values he is using. In discovering relevant values, he should turn first to the over-all cultural value system. The American culture, for example, has within it distinct patterns of values which have been described by rhetoricians and anthropologists, and these analyses should be examined by the advocate.[4] Within the culture individuals vary widely in their values, but some clues to their attitudes may be obtained from certain correlated characteristics. Membership in voluntary groups indicates value preferences, viz., political parties, religious denominations, social action groups. The socio-economic class of the individual will also be associated with general attitudes. Sex differences also indicate certain values because of the different roles played by men and women in our country.

B. *What information about your subject do they have?* The advocate must particularly estimate what the audience already knows and what it will accept as fact. This material he may use as evidence for his basic arguments. To discover this he must consider what the audience has been exposed to. Their general level and type of education will imply certain area or background levels of information. The social context of the advocate's topic will be another clue. If it is a subject recently in the news, the audience will more likely be aware of information about it. Voluntary audiences are usually mixed in this respect; many are interested and come to learn; others already have much information and come because they are interested. Basically, the amount of information the audience has is dependent on its interest and experience with the subject, and the advocate should analyze the various occasions and activities which make up each of these factors for the particular audience.

C. What general principles will the audience accept? We have separated our discussion of warrants from information in general because warrants are of a different nature and so should receive separate evaluation. Here we refer to warrants which the audience will accept. These are general principles relating one event to another, or relating values, definitions, and purposes to each other and to events. We suggest that the best procedure for the advocate to follow in audience analysis is to construct his arguments and then evaluate each warrant, deciding if the warrant requires backing or if the audience will accept it. Experiences and value systems both lead to warrants, and the methods of investigating these have already been described.

D. What relevant experiences has the audience had? This is not a repetition of the previous questions, but instead asks what personal experiences have the members of the audience had which can be used to create personal involvement with your position on the proposition? Has one of them been a victim of a robbery? Is one a newspaper reporter or publisher? Who is acquainted with the blood bank? Who has been in the armed services? Do any speak a foreign language? Have any been abroad? Are they in business? the professions? If the advocate will investigate what personal experiences are relevant to his proposition, he can use these in constructing his arguments to make them more significant and meaningful for individuals in his audience.

E. What does the audience think of the advocate? Their attitude toward the speaker will determine what consideration they will give to his discourse and what statements they will accept without requiring support. If the audience thinks the advocate has special knowledge, training, or experience, then they will give his words more weight than if they believe he has no special competence. In the latter case, it may be wise for the advocate to indicate his qualifications on the subject (subtly, of course) and to give special care to explaining his arguments. The question of what the audience will accept on faith is important. In general, it seems accurate to say that an audience will accept any information as true unless it has reason to disbelieve or doubt the information or the advocate. Even if the audience is in disagreement with the advocate's position on the proposition, it will usually believe his assertions of fact unless the information conflicts greatly with other beliefs or common sense. If the audience thinks, for example, that the writer, the speaker, or the sponsor is excessively biased (not just in disagreement with them), it may regard the information presented as biased, whether it is or not. In such an event, the advocate should take exceptional care to use accurate evidence and careful documentation.[5]

ORGANIZING THE PROOF

Propositions of belief can be proved directly by the processes of reasoning described in Chapter five. Usually there is one over-all argument leading directly to the proposition and the elements of this argument are further supported by sub-arguments. The over-all argument states the issues and the sub-arguments are contentions in support of the issues. Let us return to one of the propositions in Chapter three, "Mr. X is guilty of embezzlement." To prove the affirmative the advocate must present proof that Mr. X "willfully misappropriated property without the consent of the owner for his own personal use." The phrase in quotation marks states the criteria of definition for the term "embezzlement," and thus the over-all argument is one of reasoning from characteristics to description. To prove the proposition, the advocate must present evidence that fits into the definition: How much money was it? Did he actually take it? Was it an accident or a deliberate theft? How was the money used? Each of the four issues must be established by arguments on the basis of evidence in the actual case under consideration. On the top of p. 217 are examples of arguments on two issues.

Each one of the issues must be established for the proposition to be established. If any issue is not proved, then the proposition is not proved. And the issues are established by treating them as conclusions and supporting them with evidence and warrants. This process may go back several arguments, so that there is a chain of arguments leading to a conclusion. Another illustration of this is the argument in Chapter five drawn from the Supreme Court decision in *Brown v. Topeka Board of Education.* (See p. 217, bottom.) Some chain arguments may be quite long, but in every case the individual units of argument will have evidence, warrant, and conclusion, and they can be evaluated independently.

Another aspect of case building to note is that independent lines of reasoning may lead to the same conclusion. We may, for example, use three reasoning processes to support the conclusion "the corn crop of Dullnia is failing."

1. Dullnia is buying corn on the world market. (Reasoning from effect to cause.)
2. The testimony of an agricultural expert who visited Dullnia. (Testimonial evidence.)
3. The presence of drought and poor growing conditions this year. (Cause to effect.)

In this series of arguments rather than having a clear set of issues to be established, the proof of the proposition depends on the number and plausibility of the component ar-

Argument	Issue	Proposition
Actual bank records ⟶	X deposited $1,000 in his personal bank account. ⟶ X used the money personally. ⟶	
	X's employer testifies he did not authorize the withdrawal of the funds. ⟶ X took the money without the owner's consent. ⟶	} X embezzled $1,000.
Segregated schools separate students on the basis of color alone. ⟶	Segregated schools give Negro students inferiority feelings. ⟶	Segregated schools interfere with the education of Negro students.

guments.[6] In such cases one strong one may be sufficient, but the more independent arguments which lead to the same conclusion, the more probable is that conclusion.

Regarding these two different structures of proof, we would advise the advocate first to use as many different reasoning processes as possible to establish each conclusion, from sub-contentions to the proposition itself, giving precedence to the strongest proofs. Second, he should begin the chain of proof at the most advanced evidence which the audience will accept and move to the proposition from there.

PROPOSITIONS OF BELIEF

There are several types of propositions of belief, and we will indicate how each type may be proved using the various processes of reasoning which we described in Chapter five.

Propositions of Description. These are propositions of belief which attempt to classify, describe, or categorize an event. The following are examples of such propositions:

John cheated on his mathematics examination.
Nuclear fallout is reaching dangerous levels.
Communist China committed aggression against India.
The concept of states rights is anachronistic.
Juvenile delinquency is a serious national problem.

The principal reasoning process used to support this type of proposition is reasoning from characteristics to a description. Criteria of definition are given or assumed for the critical words in the proposition and arguments are presented to demonstrate that the characteristics of the situation satisfy the criteria. The details of the process are described in Chapters three and five. This process of description is basic to any proposition of belief, indeed any conclusion, since it is about the accuracy of language. Usually it is necessary to use other types of reasoning to establish the characteristics of the situation, and most of the case will usually be concerned with establishing the facts of the situation through testimony, cause-to-effect reasoning, argument from example to generalization, etc.

The proposition of description may also be supported by presenting comparisons, in which the parallel cases show similar characteristics, and the conclusion is that they should be described in the same way. A further method of support is to present opinion testimony from an authority who states that the description is appropriate. The authority must be an expert witness and is subject to the tests of opinion evidence described in Chapter four.

Propositions Establishing Existence. These propositions of belief assert the physical existence of an event, condition, or relationship. Examples are:

Broken homes usually result in neurotic children.
Southern states spend less on education than do Northern states.
X country is arming for aggression.
The political rift between X and Y country is widening.
M killed N.
Dullnia's corn crop is failing.

If the proposition asserts a general condition or relationship, then it usually can be established by reasoning from examples to a causal or descriptive generalization. The conclusions of arguments from examples are general principles or patterns, and these principles are often used as warrants in other arguments. If the proposition asserts the existence of a particular event or condition (as do the last four of the sample propositions), then arguments with causal warrants are most relevant: reasoning from cause to effect supports a prediction; reasoning from effect to cause establishes an event in the present or past, as does reasoning from circumstantial evidence to a hypothesis. Of course, argument from cause to effect may also be used when the entire relationship is in the past, for example in showing that:

M had a motive for killing N (cause). ⟶ Therefore, M probably killed N (effect).

People with motives for killing another often do kill him.

Arguments from comparison can also be used to assert the existence of events by demonstrating that similar situations involve such relationships or characteristics, e.g., from our experience with a previous expansion of the social security program, we can predict the effect which will result from a new expansion of the same program. Of course, reasoning from analogy may also be used to establish relationships or events, e.g., analogies which compare the human body to a machine may suggest the existence of certain mechanisms. And as always, direct opinion evidence may assert the existence of an event or a relationship.

Propositions Making Value Judgments. Examples of these are:

The United Nations is beneficial to the United States.
Capitalism is superior to socialism.
Contraceptives are moral.
Freedom of speech is a valuable right.
Killing people is wrong.
Dropping the atomic bomb on Japan was wrong.

Sometimes a value judgment stands alone: The *New York Times* is a good newspaper. At other times it is a concealed directive: Freedom of speech is good; health is good. These latter carry with them an implicit command to try to achieve them. We would think it peculiar for a judge to uphold the goodness of freedom of speech and at the same time make a ruling prohibiting it. The major process of argument used to support value propositions is the one we have described as reasoning from characteristics to a value judgment. The process applies to both of the kinds of propositions we have just described. In the first type, the evidence consists of component characteristics of the event, e.g., attributes of the *New York Times*. In the second type of proposition, the evidence usually consists of effects of the event, e.g., consequences of freedom of speech.

Values can also be supported through reference to comparisons in which the same value system is operating on similar situations. For example, the revolution of an underdeveloped nation can be given a positive value by comparing it to the American Revolution. Likewise, analogies may throw light on a value judgment. An example of this would be: "Breakdowns in communication are as bad as sand in lubricating oil." Direct testimony may also support this proposition.

Particularly in building a case for a conclusion of value, the advocate must take his arguments back far enough to ground them in values which the audience will understand and accept. For many propositions the values of the immediate warrant leading to the conclusion will be acceptable, but on the other hand, they may have to be supported or led up to by preceding arguments. The advocate should also pay special attention to the counter-analysis of the proposition. What values will oppose the proposition and how do they relate to it? These must be overcome. For example, an argument asserting the rightness of liberal divorce laws might claim this on the basis that they would allow more happiness. Against this, however, may be held the claim that they result in instability in marriage, which is bad. The affirmative argument assigns values from a value system in which personal happiness is important; the negative argument moves from a value system based on the community or society. Ways of overcoming objections and counter arguments were noted in Chapter six, and we remind the advocate that they should always be considered in the planning of proof.

OPPOSING PROPOSITIONS OF BELIEF

Up to now most of the discussion has been how to prove the affirmative side of the proposition of belief. But what about the person opposing the proposition, the negative advocate? In all propositions of belief he has two possible approaches. He may either attack the affirmative advocate's proof or he may raise a counter-argument of his own. If the negative advocate has a clear understanding of the proof requirements of the proposition, then he can challenge the strength of the affirmative's argument wherever it is weak. In Chapter six we have indicated that the first line of attack should be on the affirmative analysis and then on the issues, remembering that the defeat of one issue is sufficient to prevent the proof of the proposition.

While attacking an opposition position is often adequate, it seems to us that the negative advocate should also uphold a position of his own and raise counter-arguments to match and overturn the arguments of his opponent. He does this by presenting evidence and reasoning to support opposite or alternative propositions. In a proposition of belief regarding a description of "negligence," the affirmative advocate must present evidence that satisfies the legal definition of negligence, and the negative advocate should not only question the affirmative evidence where possible, but should try to present proof which will remove the event from the category of "negligence" to, say, "accident." In raising a counter-description, the use of testimony and comparisons may also be useful, just as it is on the affirmative. Any argument process which is used to support a proposition of belief can also be used to support alternative conclusions for the negative advocate, whether it be for a description, factual existence, or a value judgment.

Of course, to arrive at a different conclusion the negative will either begin with different evidence or use a different warrant, or both. But like the affirmative, he should use as many methods of proof as possible to establish his position, and he should make each as strong as he can. In a real sense the negative advocate should be a positive advocate, even though he opposes the proposition under consideration. However, there are certain situations in which the negative advocate is not concerned so much with presenting a counter-position. The defense attorney in a court maintains a strictly negative position on the question of his client's guilt and need not prove that someone else committed the crime (although he does construct positive proof for many issues, e.g., his client's alibi). But usually advancing answering arguments is wise. Legislators discussing the merits of a bill, for example, present opposing value judgments about the bill's effects, though they may not offer alternative legislation. Political analysts may point to purges as a sign of a power struggle in a totalitarian government, but other analysts may interpret the purges as a sign of a revision of party doctrine.

PROPOSITIONS OF ACTION

These propositions always assert "should" or "ought to"; they are directives or imperatives regarding an action, policy, or behavior. Examples are:

Motion pictures should be censored by the government.
The United States should withdraw from the United Nations.
Homosexuality should be legalized.
Candidate Z should be elected mayor.
The Peace Corps must be extended.

Since the proposition is always phrased to advocate a change in action or commitment, the affirmative has the burden of proof to show that the action should be taken. The proof rests upon the propositions of belief which we have just described; propositions of action are based on other propositions. In essence, the action is shown to have certain consequences which are good, and to obtain the consequences we must act. Thus the problem of proof is to build up consequences which are valuable enough to justify the action. First, let us look at the general forms of reasoning used, and then we will consider three types of organization for the proof.

The action advocated is a condition which is not currently in existence. The advocate must therefore set up a hypothetical situation in which the action is assumed to exist and then he must predict the effects of that action. How does he know what the action will be? By developing a specific description of the action or plan or proposal. If he is supporting a congressional bill, for example, the legislation itself describes the specifics of the plan. If he is supporting a candidate for office, previous records and asserted intentions (platforms) may tell him what the candidate will do if elected. There may be previous action of a similar nature to look to. Finally, the advocate may be free to develop his own specific proposal within the proposition. It is important to understand exactly what the action is, because the advocate must prove that the proposal is possible, i.e., that it can operate. Some proposals may be so complicated that they will not function, or they may require cooperation from persons or groups which may not be forthcoming. The advocate should prepare proof that his proposal can be established or that the action actually can be taken. He may not need to present this proof, depending on his analysis of the audience, but he should always clearly understand the practical operation of his proposition.

The effects of the action are closely tied to the proposal itself, but we will separate them in our discussion for purposes of clarity. There are several proof processes which can be used to establish the effects of the action. The obvious process to use is argument from cause to effect. General cause-effect relations are applied to the proposal and the consequences are predicted. The importance of knowing exactly *what* the proposal is becomes clear at this point: The advocate must know what causal factors are present in the action in order to predict the consequences. Comparisons can also be used to predict the results of a proposal. It may be compared with a similar action and similar effects predicted. A candidate for office may point to his record in another office. A state law may be patterned after a similar law in another state. Finally, the opinion of authorities may enable the prediction of the consequences of the action, but this testimonial evidence should be given the firmer accompaniment of argument from cause to effect or argument from comparison.

For the action to be accepted, the consequences of the proposition must be beneficial, as we have observed in Chapter three. Often there will be no need to prove that the effects cited are good (or bad), since this will usually be accepted by the audience as self-evident. Most of the proof is concerned with establishing what the consequences are, and this usually involves consequences already accepted as beneficial by the audience. For example, in proving that the United States should join the European Common Market, the advocate would try to prove that doing so would lead to greater foreign markets for U. S. industry, lower prices for U. S. consumers, savings to exporters, etc. These are consequences which most audiences would accept as benefits, and what the advocate must do is demonstrate how they follow from his proposal. If the value of the consequences is doubted by the audience, then the advocate must establish their positive value with the methods described earlier under proof of value judgments. The values which are used to support propositions of action must be of appropriate magnitude to the proposal. Values supporting social action are concerned with the worth and significance of social needs, not with a single individual's personal preference. Military actions, for instance, are based on military goals, which in turn may be rooted in national goals and values. Generally, we can say that the system of values is no less circumscribed than the context of the action supported, and often is much larger. Thus we may argue that the public schools in our district should teach reading by the phonics method because we want our children to learn to read well (values relating to local school, community, and family), or because we are in competition with the enemy in education (national and international values), or because every person has the right to read well and have access to our cultural heritage (human and cultural values).

But a question may have arisen about the beneficial consequences of the proposition. What if some of the consequences are not beneficial and are downright dangerous? This is what the negative advocate attempts to show, that the harmful consequences of the proposal outweigh the beneficial aspects. In his counter-analysis the affirmative advocate must consider what objections might be brought in this manner against the proposition. He can defend against a harmful consequence in three ways. (1) He can modify the proposal so that it will not have the harmful effect, either by eliminating or interfering with a causal factor in the action. (2) The advocate can refute the attack, contending that the harmful consequence will not result from his proposal. (3) He may overbalance with advantages any disadvantages of the action, demonstrating that the benefits are more important and extensive.

Thus propositions of action are proved by linking the proposal to significant beneficial consequences and supporting these, if necessary, against any disadvantages. Three general methods of organizing the arguments seem most useful. The choice among the three should be determined by both the analysis of the proposition and by the analysis of the audience.

1 / *Explanation of Benefits*

This is often the simplest and the most direct proof of a proposition of action. The advocate lists and proves the benefits which will result from his proposition. Of course, he will want to concentrate on the most important of the consequences and show how they follow from the proposition. Many types of benefits are amenable to this treatment. For example, one effect of the proposal may provide a good condition which was not provided before; another effect may be good because it solves a problem; another consequence may be beneficial because it remedies an injustice; another because it furthers achievement of a goal, etc. Here is an example of this organization of arguments.

The United States should remove its tariff barriers to imports, because:

U. S. foreign economic aid could be reduced.
This would solve our balance of payments problem.
Economic development of underdeveloped countries would be encouraged.
U. S. citizens would receive lower prices on many products.
International good will would follow.

Each one of these contentions demonstrates a beneficial effect of the action, and each one must be proved by the advocate, who hopes that all of them together establish enough benefit to justify the action. Of course, depending on the proposition, the advocate may have to explain a more or less detailed program to demonstrate what the action consists of and how it would work. In addition, he must be prepared to defend his proposal against disadvantages the audience may think of or an opponent may present. The number of benefits presented by the advocate depends upon the proposition. Sometimes only one major argument will be presented, and sometimes several may be used. In all cases the advocate should choose the most important arguments for the first and most careful proof. The importance of an argument depends upon the values with which it is linked. The more important the values in the context of the subject matter, the more significant the argument.

2 / Solving a Problem

This is perhaps the most "motivating" of the three approaches to proving propositions of action given here. The first half of the proof of the proposition establishes the presence of a problem, and the second half of the proof demonstrates that the action will solve it. Thus the proposal is proved beneficial because it solves a serious problem. In our culture the presence of a problem is a strong incentive to find a solution, and the more serious the problem is, the more motivation there is to accept the proposal as a solution. In short, the more serious the problem, the more beneficial the solution.

Birth control information should be distributed as part of U. S. technical foreign aid, because:

The increase in world population, especially in the underdeveloped countries, will create serious problems to those countries and to the rest of the world.

The dissemination of birth control information as a part of U. S. technical aid will increase the use of birth control, which will help control the increase in population.

Movies should be censored because:

Lewd motion pictures are destroying the morals of youth.

Censorship will eliminate lewd motion pictures and their effect on morals.

Establishing that a problem exists depends on the three types of propositions of belief. To prove that the situation is a problem requires a general definition of a problem (reasoning from characteristics to a description). To prove that the necessary circumstances exist requires the methods described for propositions asserting existence. To prove that these circumstances are harmful uses methods of proof for value judgments. Usually the major emphasis of the advocate's argument is on the second of these components, which attempts to prove the existence of circumstances which will justify the designation of "problem." Usually the circumstances themselves carry values with them, but occasionally it will be necessary to demonstrate specific harm or danger resulting from the condition. For example, even if an advocate proves that there are not enough high school teachers to staff the nation's high schools, he has not proved that harm results to the nation from the situation. Therefore, unless the audience accepts the judgment that this is harmful, the advocate must demonstrate the resultant harm or else there is no reason to call the situation a problem. Another aspect to note is that the harm must be comparable in magnitude to the action demanded. Rarely is an action justified which disarranges the lives of many persons for the benefit of a very few unless the wrong is grave indeed. This is probably the basic reason why the logical presumption in a proposition of action is with the current situation; it is too much trouble to change the present system without good reason.

The exact nature of the problem should be analyzed by the advocate. Its extent, causes, and effects are all relevant to what he must prove. Particularly important are the causal relations of the situation, since it is on these that the solution must operate. Most of the argument required to prove a problem, since it involves asserting existence of situations, will be causal. This should not be confused with the identification of the causal forces operating to bring about the situation or the effects of a situation. For example, reasoning from example to generalization may establish the existence of juvenile delinquency in urban areas.

Then argument from cause to effect may prove that a large portion of this can be caused by immoral books and motion pictures. Thus the advocate has established the existence of a causal relation within the problem situation: "Dirty books cause juvenile delinquency." In presenting a solution he will try to reduce the problem by reducing one of the causes.[7]

The action may solve the problem in three ways. First, it may remove a cause that is producing the problem, as a removal of trade barriers will allow underdeveloped nations to sell more of certain goods abroad. Second, it may introduce a new causal factor, whose effects will be the solution, as: "National health insurance will allow insurance coverage for all U. S. citizens." Third, it may counteract one cause with another which will prevent the harmful effects, as: "The buying of farm surpluses will raise the low market price caused by overproduction." The advocate should be certain of the exact causal relationship between the solution and the problem, because on this depends his claim of beneficial consequences.[8]

As with all argument, the process should be adapted to the knowledge and experience of the audience. If they are already aware of the problem—its harm and extent—the advocate need not devote extensive proof to this conclusion. Even so, it is wise to present enough analysis of the problem to the audience so that the operation of the solution will be clear. Also it is important to explain how, with proof, the proposal will solve the problem. Too often we have heard advocates devote most of their time proving a problem exists and then present the proposal like a magician flourishing his magic wand over the halved woman, but fail to establish that the proposal would remedy the situation. They do not show the lovely lady restored to health, happiness, and wholeness. The advocate may also wish to combine this approach with the first type of case and contend that his proposition will remedy a problem and have additional benefits.[9]

3 / *Comparing Alternative Courses of Action*

Especially when the proposal is a substitute for or change in an existing policy or plan, the advocate may prove its beneficial consequences by comparing it with the consequences of the plan it is to replace. The proof consists of presenting advantages not possible under the *status quo* or comparative advantages, i.e., bigger and better benefits.

The third edition of *Webster's New International Dictionary* should be used instead of the second edition.
> The third has more entries than the second.
> The third is more accurately descriptive than the second.
> The third includes more meanings than does the second.

If you buy a low-priced automobile, you should buy a Frappé.
(Here follows a list of a series of tests, in which the Frappé was proved superior in every way to the other low-priced cars.)

The use of comparisons can also be applied when a choice must be made from several alternative programs. One proposal is supported by eliminating the alternative or by showing that one is more advantageous than another. In this it is obviously essential to present advantages of the proposition besides eliminating the other possible choices, because eliminating alternatives is insufficient to show that the final alternative is beneficial. Thus the best approach here is a combination of elimination and comparative advantages.

The specific comparisons are usually in relation to goals, solutions, or benefits which are similar among the proposals. For example, the choices might be among various remedies to a problem, and the actions are compared to discover which one will solve the problem best. So the advocate should discover what the goals or effects of the proposals are and then make the comparisons on these relevant issues. Closer to the surface in this than in the previous methods of organization are the value judgments implicit in the proposition of action. The advantages which are compared are always consequences attached to value preferences.

OPPOSING PROPOSITIONS OF ACTION

Three general areas of argument are open to the opponent of the proposition of policy. The first is that he may attack the proof for the case, contending that the affirmative advocate has failed to establish reasonable arguments. If the affirmative uses a simple description of benefits, the negative advocate can attack the causal relations, denying that the effects will be produced. Or he can attack the amount of benefit, denying that the advantages are of consequence. If the affirmative presents his proposal as a solution to a problem, the negative advocate can first attack the problem, refuting its existence, extent, or harmfulness. The negative should carefully examine the proposal as a solution to determine *how* it is supposed to remedy the evil and *if* it actually does so. The action should be viewed as a cause, and its efficacy as an adequate solution should be evaluated. If the affirmative position is one of comparative advantages, the negative may refute alleged disadvantages of a rejected proposal and refute the advantages of the affirmative proposition. In addition, it may be possible to point out an alternative which the affirmative position overlooks, or a combination of alternatives which may be more beneficial than any one alone. Our discussion of affirmative cases indicates where they must be proved; they can be attacked at the same points. As with propositions of belief, the negative can logically defeat the proposition by defeating one of the issues.

The negative position should not be one of refutation only, but should be combined with two other types of arguments, the raising of objections to the affirmative proposal and the maintaining of an alternative action in preference to the affirmative action. The negative objections to the affirmative proposal may be either that it is unworkable or that it will have undesirable consequences. Proving that the action is impossible requires cause-to-effect reasoning. The advocate may prove that the machinery would be too complex to operate or that technical skills are not adequate to develop some proposal or that the administration is inadequate, etc. In establishing these arguments, the advocate must be specific and as thorough as possible, not asserting, but proving with evidence, warrant, and conclusion that the action is impossible. On the other hand, to raise disadvantages to the proposition usually assumes that it will operate to some extent (even if just enough to create problems). The evils of the proposal are established in the same way as the advantages; the action is proved to result in effects linked with values, in this case negative values. The same reasoning processes (cause-to-effect, comparison, testimony) can be used to predict effects, and these effects should be ones which the audience will accept as detriments.

> The United States should not remove its tariff barriers.
> > Industries now protected would be damaged.
> > The economy would be harmed because of decreased sales and employment.
> > The government would lose tariff revenues.
> > Industries vital to national defense would be damaged.

These counter-arguments are presented to overbalance the benefits which are claimed for the affirmative's proposition. Obviously, the negative advocate should combine his arguments to both refute the advantages claimed for the proposal and to prove its disadvantages.

The third class of arguments which should be used by the negative advocate is really an affirmation of a positive position: He should stand for an alternative choice of action in opposition to the action asked for by the proposition. Usually the negative advocate is upholding the current situation, the *status quo*. This is because of his attack of the affirmative action. Denying that a problem is present or that the affirmative proposal has advantages places the negative in agreement with things as they are. It seems wise for him to develop this stand as a positive choice, pointing out its benefits. If the affirmative presents a problem, the negative may even admit to it but demonstrate that it can be solved using methods already available. The negative may need to extend his position to a modification of the present system in order to deal with the affirmative position. In this case he may agree that some problems or inadequacies exist, but he presents methods of solving them which are simply modifications in methods or mechanisms now in effect. Or similarly, modifications in the *status quo* may create additional advantages to match the advantages of an affirmative proposal. In some cases the negative advocate may completely revise the *status quo*, but in a different way than the affirmative, thus in effect proposing an alternative proposition of action. Especially in a modification or total alteration of the *status quo* the negative advocate demonstrates the comparative benefits of his position by attacking the affirmative proposition and raising objections to it. And he should further support his own position as a proposition of action itself, showing its workability and beneficial consequences. Whatever the position of the negative, it should be an outgrowth of his analysis of the proposition, and should be based on what he believes to be the reasonable conclusion about the proposition.

Unfortunately we cannot claim that this is a complete explanation of making evidence and reasoning processes into persuasive proof for propositions. There are types of propositions for which we have not described the processes of proof; there are untold subtleties of proof involved in the cases we have briefly described here; and every advo-

cate knows that propositions, reasoning, and evidence combine in the most complex and tangled ways one can imagine.
But the relationships which we have described indicate
some fundamental ways of discovering and fulfilling the
requirements of proof for rational conclusions. With these
as basic methods, the advocate can approach argument
and advocacy with insight.

►NOTES◄

1. This definition of proof is a long-used one, and one
   which has important implications. Aristotle's *Rhetoric*
   implicitly uses this definition and includes not only the
   arguments as proof, but also the character of the
   speaker and the emotions linked to the proposition.
   Richard Whately, in *Elements of Rhetoric* (1828),
   made a distinction between logic, which he described
   as investigative and evaluative, and proof, which was
   reasoning made persuasive to an audience. Today in
   argumentation theory the distinction is not generally
   made, but it is a useful one to indicate that "objective"
   arguments must be adapted to their audience if they
   are to be persuasive.
2. In many cases, perhaps most, warrants are assumptions
   which are held in common by the audience and the advocate, so he need not make them explicit in stating
   the argument. However, when the warrant itself may
   be challenged—as in argument by criteria of definition
   —it may require explicit statement and even proof of
   its correctness.
3. This effect is discussed by Kurt Lang and Gladys Engel
   Lang, "Reactions of Viewers," in Sidney Kraus (ed.),
   The Great Debates (Bloomington, Ind.: Indiana University Press, 1962), pp. 313-330.
4. See Chapter eight, "Winning Belief through Wants and
   Values," in Wayne C. Minnick, *The Art of Persuasion*
   (Boston: Houghton-Mifflin Company, 1957), pp. 198-

222. Another formulation of American values is in Edward Steele and Charles Redding, "The American Value System," *Western Speech* (Spring, 1962), pp. 83-91.

5. Experimental research on these effects is described in Chapter two, "Credibility of the Communicator," in Carl I. Hovland, Irving L. Janis, and Harold H. Kelley, *Communication and Persuasion* (New Haven: Yale University Press, 1953), pp. 19-55.

6. In propositions asserting the existence of events, things, conditions, or relations there will not be a distinct set of issues. Instead, the proof of the proposition will depend upon the strength of the arguments which lead to its assertion.

7. For suggestions on the proof of problems and causes, see Chapter eight, "Thinking and Speaking about Problems," and Chapter nine, "Thinking and Speaking about Causes," in Otis Walter and Robert Scott, *Thinking and Speaking* (New York: The Macmillan Company, 1962), pp. 119-133.

8. For suggestions on the proof of solutions, see Chapter ten, "Thinking and Speaking about Solutions," in *ibid.*, pp. 148-157.

9. This problem-solution-benefits pattern is the presentation most often used in intercollegiate debate, and most textbooks on this activity analyze the approach in detail. See Chapters four and five in Arthur Kruger, *Modern Debate* (New York: McGraw-Hill Book Company, 1960), pp. 37-77.

► E X E R C I S E S ◄

1. Examine one of the following to discover (1) the proposition under consideration, (2) the affirmative case presented in support of the proposition, (3) the persuasive qualities of the proof. Your views may be presented in class discussion or a paper.

a. Douglas MacArthur, "Address to Congress," in Carroll Arnold, Douglas Ehninger, and John Gerber (eds.), *Speaker's Resource Book* (Chicago: Scott, Foresman and Company, 1961), pp. 275-280.

b. Ralph Zimmerman, "Mingled Blood," in *ibid.*, pp. 99-101.

c. Henry B. DuPont, "The Greatest Invention of Them All," in *ibid.*, pp. 193-197.

d. Thomas Waring, "The Southern Case against Desegregation," in William Petersen and David Matza (eds.), *Social Controversy* (Belmont, Calif.: Wadsworth, 1963), pp. 175-183, or in *Harper's Magazine* (January, 1956), pp. 39-45.

e. Robert Lekachman, "The Case for the Primacy of the Public Schools," in Petersen, *op. cit.*, pp. 75-86.

f. William J. Gibbons, S. J., "The Catholic Value System and Human Fertility," in *ibid.*, pp. 15-29.

g. The first and second affirmative constructive speeches in the 1959 West Point final debate by William Welsh and Richard Kirshberg, in Russel Windes and Arthur Kruger, *Championship Debating* (Portland, Me.: J. Weston Walch, 1961), 82 ff.

h. Hans Küng, "Latin: The Church's Mother Tongue?" *Harper's Magazine* (October, 1963), pp. 60-64.

2. Describe and evaluate the evidence, arguments, cases, and persuasive methods for the affirmative and negative sides in these debates:

a. Any debate selected from *Championship Debating*.

b. The debate over extra-sensory perception in *Science* (August 26, 1955 and January 6, 1956).

c. The debate over the theories of Immanuel Velikovsky, in these two articles and the letters to the editor in subsequent issues of *Harper's Magazine*. Eric Larrabee, "Scientists in Collision: Was Veli-

kovsky Right?" *Harper's Magazine* (August, 1963),
pp. 48-55; Donald H. Menzel, "The Debate over
Velikovsky," *Harper's Magazine* (December,
1963), pp. 83-86.

d. The debate over the third edition of *Webster's
New International Dictionary* in Wilson Follett,
"Sabotage in Springfield," *Atlantic Monthly* (January, 1962), pp. 73-77 and in Bergen Evans, "But
What's a Dictionary For?" *Atlantic Monthly*
(May, 1962), pp. 57-62.

e. The first Nixon-Kennedy debate in the 1960 Presidential campaign, in Sidney Kraus (ed.), *The
Great Debates* (Bloomington, Ind.: Indiana University Press, 1962), pp. 348-368.

f. The first Lincoln-Douglas debate in 1858, in Paul
Angle (ed.), *Created Equal?* (Chicago: The University of Chicago Press, 1958), pp. 103-137.

3. Prepare and present an eight- to ten-minute speech
proving a proposition of belief. Make your case persuasive.

4. Prepare and present an eight- to ten-minute speech
proving a proposition of action. Make your case persuasive.

5. Write an essay of advocacy on either side of a proposition arising from a controversy. Create a persuasive
case for a particular audience.

6. Present a debate on a proposition of belief or action
using one of these formats.

For one speaker on each side

Affirmative	—Eight minutes (to present his case)
Negative	—Ten minutes (refutation and negative case)
Affirmative	—Two minutes (refutation and summary)

For two speakers (classroom debate)

| First affirmative | —Five minutes (beginning proof of proposition) |

First negative	—Five minutes (refutation and negative case)
Second affirmative	—Five minutes (refutation and completion of case)
Second negative	—Five minutes (refutation and completion of case)

Cross-examination: The first speaker on each side cross-examines the opposing speakers for three minutes, with the negative beginning the question period.

| Second negative | —Three minutes (summary) |
| Second affirmative | —Three minutes (summary) |

For two speakers (intercollegiate debate format)

Constructive speeches:

First affirmative	—Ten minutes
First negative	—Ten minutes
Second affirmative	—Ten minutes
Second negative	—Ten minutes

Rebuttal speeches:

First negative	—Five minutes
First affirmaitve	—Five minutes
Second negative	—Five minutes
Second affirmative	—Five minutes

SUBJECT INDEX

NAME INDEX

7044